Hedges and Ground Cover for Your Garden

生垣とカバープランツ

写真＝鈴木おさむ　文＝相関芳郎

はじめに

　人は日常の家庭生活の場として家を求め，周囲には敷地を持つことを望んでいる。そして，その保守のためには家屋も部屋も壁で区切られているし，敷地は境界線を定めて囲い，外部からの侵入を防いできている。

　さて，その敷地の保全のためには柵や塀，垣根などを巡らすことが古くから行われてきた。漢字の籬（まがき）とはそれらの外柵のことであるが，これは，間囲う，間塞（ませ）に由っているという。

　そして，その敷地内には庭を意味する園が囲まれ，農作物の生産をしたり，植物を植えて，自然環境を身近かに造ることがなされてきている。ちなみに園という字は，囲いの中に袁（「衣が長い」意味）があるように，その内部で長い衣服を着て悠然と暮らすさまを示している。

　その庭園が各様の外柵の変遷を経て，生きた植物による生垣が作られるようになったのは何時頃からのことであろうか。その始源について知ることは難しいことであるが，その発生の一つとして，境界地に線引きをして所々に付近の生きた枝を挿し込んでおいたものが，地下に根を出して生育し，結果的に生垣になったと思いめぐらすのも楽しさが増してくることである。のちには手頃な大きさの山野の木を探してきて植えたかも知れないし，直接種子を播くように進歩したとも思えてくる。

　生垣は土塀や石積み，板や竹張りなどと違って生命があり，生育しての緑視感は目や気持を和らげてくれる美観性がある。管理に手間のかかることもあるが，その設置の労力や経費が他の塀や柵に比べて少なくて済み，身近かに緑の成長を見る楽しみを長く味わうことができる。

　生垣の再認識は，17年前の昭和53年の仙台沖地震での軽量ブロック塀崩壊の事故の結果から真剣に考えられはじめた。ブロック塀から生垣への改造，管理などの補助指導をする自治体がふえてきている。

　鈴木おさむ氏は写真家としての眼で生垣の現況を撮られ，拝見すると，このたびの阪神・淡路大震災のこともあり，改めて生垣の存在価値も増した。その

中には普遍的なものをはじめとして，準生垣的と考えられる植栽様式も含まれている。併せて説明を加えておきたい。

　生垣を囲う線，区切る線とすれば，その内部には面としての庭がある。そのほぼ平面的な地域内には木立・草花などの植物，庭石ほかの立体的な存在と共に広場や園路があり，また芝や笹などの平坦的な植栽地がある。そして近年は，緑被面積を増加するために地被植物（グラウンド・カバー・プランツ）利用の傾向が高まってきている。なお，都市内や高速道などでの緑化向上などの見地からもその関心度が高い。

　地上を低く這う蔓性種と地下茎を横走する諸種の地被植物と共に，建物の壁面緑化，棚による上面緑化などの各種の被覆植物も記しておきたい。

　また，庭の下部には諸所に少量ながら草本類が点在して，一般樹木に比べて楚々として優雅な趣きを味わわせてくれる下草がある。その１カ所での植栽量は数株どまりであり，面積的に極めて少数である。しかも樹下や庭石，舗石の傍らなどで地面上とのつらなり役をしながら優美な動きさえ示していてくれる。日本庭園では特にその味わい深さが多いが，洋庭向きの種類も併せて挙げてみたい。

　小規模ではあったが，昭和27年に東京都井の頭自然文化園で，生垣展を催したことがあった。また同39年からは日本庭園の管理に関わり，下草や地被植物に興味を覚えはじめたことが思い出されてくる。

　終りに出版社の岡本編集部長に再三お世話になり，厚くお礼申し上げる。

平成9年3月

相関芳郎

Preface

Human beings desire a house to live in, as well as a surrounding plot of land. Just as a house is set off from the external environment by its exterior walls, the plot often has a border of some sort — a fence, wall, or hedge —to prevent intrusions from the outside. Part of the land is often arranged as a garden, where plants are cultivated for both visual pleasure and food in an effort to create a natural environment close to home.

How and when did ordinary walls and fences come to be replaced by hedges, or "living fences," as the Japanese word translates literally? This is difficult to determine. Perhaps early gardeners drew a line in the soil and inserted along the line small branches from nearby shrubs to set off their land, and the cuttings developed roots and eventually grew into what today we would call a hedge. Later, perhaps, wild plants of an appropriate size were dug up and replanted along land borders, or seeds sown directly to make a hedge.

Unlike walls of earth or stone, and board or bamboo fences, hedges are alive, their greenness and beauty engendering visual and spiritual calm. Although their upkeep takes some effort, planting a hedge requires less labor and cost than building a wall or fence, and one can then sit back and enjoy watching them grow over the years.

In Japan the value of hedges was rediscovered in 1978 following an earthquake in which lightweight-block walls collapsed, causing injury to people. Moreover, because hedges are alive, open, and natural, many municipalities began providing guidance on their growth and care.

Osamu Suzuki provides us with a photographic view of hedges in today's Japan. Looking through his manuscript in light of the recent Hanshin-Awaji Earthquake, I again realized the expanding value of hedges in our environment.

Mr. Suzuki also describes and depicts other types of plantings that are finding broader acceptance among Japanese gardeners. Gardens traditionally have been planted with various trees, shrubs, flowers, and grasses and often include walks and patios of stone. A more recent development has been ground cover, whose use has steadily been gaining adherents. Ground covers are also used in cities and along highways as a means of enhancing the greenness of the landscape. A similar development has been the use of vines and vinelike plants to cover the ground, as well as garden and building walls.

Finally, small herbaceous plants classified as undergrowth (distinguished from ground cover in that they grow singly or in clumps, but do not spread, as ground cover does) are used to add a graceful, elegant touch to gardens. Planted under trees and garden rocks, and along pavement stones, undergrowth plays a unifying, connecting role in a garden. Numerous types of undergrowth are extremely tasteful in a Japanese garden, but there also exist many varieties appropriate to Western-style gardens, and these are also introduced in this book.

In 1952 a small-scale exhibit of hedges was held at the Inokashira Shizen Bunka En garden, in Tokyo. I also remember that it was in 1964 that I began to involve myself in the care of Japanese gardens, at which time I also first became interested in ground covers and undergrowth.

In conclusion, I would like to express my deepest gratitude to the publisher for bringing this book to completion.

March 1997
Yoshiro Aizeki

目 次

はじめに ———————————————————————————— 2

生垣
    1．生垣の変遷 ———————————————————————— 10
    2．生垣の機能と利用 —————————————————————— 10
    3．生垣の種別 ———————————————————————— 11
    4．生垣の造成 ———————————————————————— 11
    5．生垣の植え付け —————————————————————— 11
    6．生垣の完成まで —————————————————————— 12
    7．完成後の管理 ——————————————————————— 12

高生垣 ———————————————————————————— 16
並生垣 ———————————————————————————— 26
中生垣 ———————————————————————————— 34
低生垣 ———————————————————————————— 44
蔓生垣 ———————————————————————————— 48
半自然形 —————————————————————————— 54
自然形 ——————————————————————————— 58
列植 ———————————————————————————— 60
すそ植え —————————————————————————— 70
二段垣 ——————————————————————————— 74
混ぜ垣 ——————————————————————————— 75

カバープランツ
    ［Ⅰ］蔓植物について ————————————————————— 78
    1．形態の種類 ———————————————————————— 78
    2．蔓植物の利用 ——————————————————————— 78
    ［Ⅱ］被覆植物について ———————————————————— 78

地被類 ——————————————————————————— 82
壁被類 ——————————————————————————— 107
上被類 ——————————————————————————— 115

下草
    下草類 ——————————————————————————— 120

索引 ———————————————————————————— 129

CONTENTS

Preface —————————————————————————————————————— 4

HEDGES
    〈A〉 Brief History of Hedges ————————————————————— 13
    〈B〉 Functions and Uses of Hedges ——————————————— 13
    〈C〉 Classification of Hedges ————————————————————— 14
    〈D〉 Selecting Plants for a Hedge —————————————————— 14
    〈E〉 Planting Hedges ——————————————————————————— 14
    〈F〉 Care Until Hedge Are Fully Grown ——————————— 15
    〈G〉 Care When Hedges Are Fully Grown ———————————— 15

Tall Hedges ——————————————————————————————————— 16
Standard-Height Hedges ——————————————————————————— 26
Medium-Short Hedges ————————————————————————————— 34
Short Hedges ——————————————————————————————————— 44
Vine Hedges ——————————————————————————————————— 48
Semi-Natural Hedges ————————————————————————————— 54
Natural Hedges ————————————————————————————————— 58
Hedgerows ——————————————————————————————————— 60
Apron Hedges ————————————————————————————————— 70
Two-Tiered Hedges —————————————————————————————— 74
Mixed Hedges ————————————————————————————————— 75

GROUND COVER
    [I] Vines and Vinelike Plants ——————————————————— 80
        〈A〉 Types of Vinelike Plants ——————————————— 80
        〈B〉 Uses of Vine Plants —————————————————— 80
    [II] Ground Cover and Other Covering Plants —————————— 80
        〈A〉 Ground Cover ——————————————————————— 80
        〈B〉 Wall-Covering Plants ————————————————— 81
        〈C〉 Planting Hung Overhead ————————————————— 81
        〈D〉 Planting and Maintenance ———————————————— 81

Ground Cover ————————————————————————————————— 82
Wall-Covering Plants ————————————————————————————— 107
Trellis Plants —————————————————————————————————— 115

UNDERGROWTH
    Undergrowth ————————————————————————————————— 121

INDEX —————————————————————————————————————— 131

Hedges and Ground Cover for Your Garden

Translation into English : Jay Thomas
Design & Layout : Kenichi Yanagawa

First Edition, July 1997
ISBN4-7661-0973-2

Graphic-sha Publishing Co., Ltd.
1-9-12 Kudan-kita, Chiyoda-ku, Tokyo 102 Japan

Phone 03-3263-4310
Fax 03-3263-5297

Printed in Hong Kong.

ヒマラヤスギ（埼玉県・花植木センター）　Deodar (*Cedrus deodara*), Saitama Prefectural Garden Plants Center

生 垣
HEDGES

1. 生垣の変遷

生垣の前提になる列状植栽はヨーロッパブドウの栽培風景から知ることができる。葡萄酒を醸造した歴史は古く、紀元前数千年頃からとされているが、同1500年頃の古代エジプトの墓地の壁面には、その収穫風景が描かれ、蔓性であるブドウが直列植栽されている。

時代が下がり、西暦79年にベスビアス山の噴火で埋没したポンペイでは、発掘調査により上流階級の住居の壁画(第1図)に、格子垣(トレリス)やパーゴラに蔓植物がまとう庭の風景があり、中産階級のルーフガーデン(屋上庭園)にもやはり蔓物をからませたパーゴラが見られている。

またローマには「刈り込み人」がいて、庭内のセイヨウツゲなどによる、動物たちの形を刈り込むトピアリー技術が行われていたという。そして生垣も設置され、その技術はイギリスに渡り16〜17世紀には広く普及したようである。

わが国では『古事記』に、「八雲立つ出雲八重垣、妻籠みに、八重垣作るその八重垣を」という有名な古歌があり、また、その編記の翌年に命じられた地誌の一つである『常陸風土記』内には、香(鹿)島神宮に奉仕していた卜部氏宅の周りは、「山の木、野草を内庭の藩籬に堺し」とあり、原初的な生垣の存在を知ることができる。

『万葉集』に及ぶと葦垣、竹垣、青垣などの語が見られ、神籬、斉垣、瑞垣などの神事的な囲いと共に多用化されていたと思われる。次の2首は大伴家持の作であろうが興味深いものである。

1793　垣ほなす人の横言繁みかもあはぬ日数多く月の経ぬらむ

2530　あらたまの寸戸が竹垣編目ゆも妹し見えなば吾恋ひめやも

そしてさらに平安中期になり、『源氏物語』には芦垣、柴垣が記され、また「植ゑし垣根」「宿の垣根」の表現もある。

また『枕草子』の「見るものは」には、「道の山里めき、あはれなるに、うつぎ垣根といふ物の、いと荒々しう、おどろかしげにさし出でたる枝どもおほかるに」とあり、すでにウツギのような低木による、刈り込まない生垣が存在していたことを知ることができる。

生垣用の苗の生産を指導したのは、元禄10年(1697)に刊行された宮崎安貞による『農業全書』である。「園籬を作る法」の中でカラタチ、クコ、ウコギ、サンショウ、クチナシ、ハリスギ、コウジ、クワ、ニワザクラ、細竹の名を挙げ、はじめの3種の栽培法を記している。

江戸時代には生垣の植栽を奨励した藩が多く、スギ、ヒノキ、ヒバ、イチイ、ネズミモチ、カシ類、マキ、マツ、カラタチ、カナメモチ、ウツギ、ウコギ、クワ、シキミ、サンゴジュ、ヤナギ、タケ類などの中から選ばれたという。なかでも米沢藩主の上杉鷹山は、饑饉の折を考え、食用になるウコギの植栽を命じたことはよく知られていて、今日でもその名残りの生垣を見ることができる。またカラタチも多く各地で植えられていたが、明治以降に有刺鉄線が輸入されて、この有刺植物の代表種も大正末期から姿が減っていった。

このように生垣の樹種も時代と共に変化しながら現在に及んできている。大正12年の関東大震災により東京の市街地の植物量は減少し、市域も郊外地に広まり、樹種と植栽方式も変化していった。昭和14年の調査(『造園雑誌』6〜3、丹羽鼎三・池田綾一氏)によると、(1)本郷・小石川区(現文京区)本所・深川区(現墨田区)は生垣数が少なく、調査数の中でカラタチが39.1%と49.7%あり、サワラ、マサキが次いでいる。(2)杉並・中野は生垣戸数が多く、サワラが90%を超え、マサキ、カナメモチが次いでいる。(3)大森区(現大田区)田園調布3丁目はほとんどに生垣があり、その80%以上が石垣、土坡上に植えられ、サワラ、マサキ、タギョウショウ、カナメモチがそれぞれ10余%あり、26種以上に及んでいる。(4)以上の7調査地域内で見られた樹種は、前記以外にイブキ刈り込み、イブキ・ツツジ刈り込み、ツツジ、バラ、ドウダンツツジ、ピラカンサ、ツバキ、サンゴジュ、ヒイラギ、アオキ、アスナロ、サザンカ、シイ(高刈り)、ヒイラギモクセイ、モチ、ツルグミ、ジンチョウゲ、イヌツゲ、ヒイラギナンテン、ヒサカキ、アセビ、ヤツデが見られたと記されている。

また翌年には大阪郊外の旧称豊能郡箕面村の桜ヶ丘、桜井の2住宅地の調査(『造園雑誌』7〜2、池田綾一氏)が発表され、(1)桜ヶ丘では91%が植栽され、カイズカイブキ34.1%、カナメモチ25.3%、ピラカンサ11%であり、(2)桜井住宅地は40.9%に見られ、カイズカイブキ28.3%、カナメモチ18.5%、ギンモクセイ17.4%であった。(3)両地では、これらの他にウバメガシ、ネズミモチ、カシ、マキ、サワラ、カラタチ、スギ、バラ、マサキ、イヌツゲ、ツツジ、カヤ、ヒバ、サザンカがあり、石垣、土坡植栽が多いとも述べている。

なお調査外ではあるが、東京の杉並区辺りから西方には、強風除けのシラカシの高生垣が多く見られたことを付記しておきたい。

のちの戦災により多くの消失を来たしているが、東京都は苗圃で都民に頒布用の苗木を生産し、私も昔の新宿駅西口広場でその即売をしたことがある。トウネズミモチ、ネズミモチ、ニッコウヒバ、マサキなど生垣用で、生長の早い高さは60cm内外の苗であった。その後の経済復興で木造の建売住宅が売られだし、やはり似たような木が外周に植えられていたものである。

近年は生垣相もだいぶ変貌を遂げた。住宅の世代交替や財産譲与での分割、移住、家屋改造などにともなう存否と改良があり、樹種の交替と植栽様式の変化などもある。さらには次の項の利用の中で示すように、近年は交通施設にも生垣形態の植栽が増しているし、ボックス植えも見られる。また外国で改良された針葉樹のコニファー類という新顔の生垣も見られ、今後も増加してゆくことと思われる。

第1、2表は十分な内容ではないが、主なる生垣の種類を挙げておく。

2. 生垣の機能と利用

(1)敷地外周の囲繞と侵入防止。

(2)内外からの視的遮蔽。

(3)通風、気温、日照、遮音などの適度な緩和。

(4)防火、防風、防煙、防砂、防塵、防潮。

(5)身近な空気の浄化。

(6)修景緑化。

(7)園内の境栽と誘導用。

以上のような基本的な機能のほかにも利用効果が多い。

(8)好みの樹種の選択による新緑、若葉の紅葉、花、実、秋の紅葉の鑑賞。

(9)コンクリート構造物の隠蔽と美化。

(10)植込み地の防護、ゴミ止め。

(11)背景美化(例:野外ステージ)。

(12)歩車道間の安全防護柵の緑化。

(13)道路の中央分離帯植栽による遮光と精神的慰安。

(14)借景庭園における下部の仕切り構成。

(15)庭園内での象形表現(例:二重垣による海の波打ち模様)。

(16)食物利用(例:ウコギ、サンショウ、クコなどの葉、キンカン、ヒメユズなどの果実など)。

(17)1年生蔓性草花の短期栽培(例:アサガオ、ルコウソウ、フウセンカズラ、ツルムラサキなど)。

(18)迷路園の設置。

(19)軽量ブロック塀などの緑化(ヘデラ、ナツヅタ、イタビカズラなど)。

ポンペイの室内の壁に描かれた庭園の光景(春山行夫著『花の文化史』より)

3．生垣の種別

純生垣と生垣に準じた列状植栽は，次のような分け方ができる。

A．位置別

1．外垣

(1)**地植え垣**　敷地の地盤上に境界，仕切用として直接植えた一般的な生垣。また単なる列植様式も含むことができる。

(2)**土坡垣**　敷地の境界上に石積み，土坡を設け，その上部に低生垣，蔓生垣などを植栽する様式。

(3)**裾垣**　塀，柵，家屋に添う低生垣。

(4)**箱植え垣**　広場，路上などに，移動可能な大型長形のプラスチック，軽量コンクリート製などの箱内への生垣植栽。連続配置も可能である。

2．内垣(庭垣)

(1)庭園内に設ける生垣であり，低・中生垣が多く，簡易な仕切り，誘導，植え込み地，花壇外周など境栽的な効用をもつ。また中には並生垣，高生垣により園内の区分をしたり，迷路作り，抜け穴などの変わった様式もある。また園内のコンクリート構造物の隠蔽などにも設けられる。

(2)**屋上垣**　人工地盤の屋上庭園用であり，強風への考慮が必要である。

(3)**箱植え垣**　屋上配置，園内の誘導のほかに，テラス，ベランダ上に連続配置して緑化とプライバシーの保護向きである。

(4)**縁植え垣**　花壇外周や一般植込地の保護のための外周列植であり，低木および中木が用いられる準生垣である。

B．材料別

(1)**樹木垣**　高・中・低木があり，常緑性と落葉性，花や実を楽しめる種類もある。

(2)**竹・笹垣**　地下茎が長く伸びない種類を用いる。半自然仕立てと刈り込み型がある。

(3)**蔓生垣**　木本・草本，常緑性・落葉性があり，金網柵，四つ目垣などに絡ませるタイプが多いが，コンクリート塀に纏着させる被覆型もある。

(4)**保護(侵入防止)垣(有刺垣)**　枝や葉に刺を有する植物を植えて，外部からの侵入を防ぐ効果をもつが，近年は減少の傾向にある。

(5)**混植垣**　同列内に2種以上の樹木を植えた様式である。

(6)**草花・野菜垣**　1年草，多年草の蔓物を用いるもので短期的な季節的な存在ではあるが，花の観賞，実の収穫が楽しめる実用垣である。

C．形状別

(1)**総刈り垣**　最も普通に見られる外垣の様式であり，角刈り型は表裏両面と天端，側部を直線に刈り込む。曲線刈りは側面や天端を曲線仕上げに刈り込む様式である。

(2)**半自然垣**　各枝先を玉作り仕上げなどにしたものの列植であり，竹の腰折垣のような異形仕上げの生垣もある。

(3)**列植垣**　一般的な一体化の刈り込みをしないで，それぞれを筒型，球型，角型などに仕立てて，同間隔に列植した様式である。

(4)**蔓生垣**　蔓性の草木を柵や四つ目などに絡ませたり結束する様式である。

(5)**果樹垣**　ナシの主枝を直立させ，側枝を斜め上，水平，直立させて，美しい幾何学模様の枝配りをしての列植であり，ブドウの針金による水平段作りなどもある。

(6)**自然垣**　自然形の列植であり，樹種により高低および直立形と放射形がある。

(7)**着生生垣**　被覆植物に含まれる蔓性植物が，気根によりコンクリート塀に密着育成させ，緑化する様式である。

D．高低別

(1)**並生垣**　外部からの視線を遮ぎる高さの最も普通の外垣であり，一般に高さは1.6～2.0m程度である。

(2)**高生垣**　強風の遮断を主目的とする外垣であり，常緑樹が適当である。管理上足場が必要であり，両側にその余地を要する。

(3)**中生垣**　並生垣と低生垣の中間的な1m内外の高さであり，視界を広めて庭内の境栽や外庭ほかの囲い向きである。

(4)**低生垣**　およそ40cm内外で，土坡上や縁植え用が多い。

(5)**二段生垣**　高さの異なる生垣を並列させた二重生垣である。

E．適地別

(1)**気温差**　熱帯地から寒冷地の間にはそれぞれの適温植物が選ばれる。

(2)**日照差**　陽地，中庸地向きの樹種が多いが，半陰地にも適した種類の選択がなされる。

(3)**乾燥差**　乾燥地，中庸地，半湿地別に適した樹種が選択される。

(4)**耐風差**　強風地には根張りのよい樹種，潮風には海岸性の種類が適している。

(5)**対公害差**　煙害，防火，耐火能力と各種の都市公害への耐性も検討されるべきである。

F．観賞別

(1)**葉生垣**　言うまでもなく生垣植栽目的の主体である。観賞的な葉の状態，季節的な色彩の変化が見られる。

(2)**花生垣**　花の美しい種類が植えられる。

(3)**実生垣**　花後に特に美しい実を結ぶ種類の生垣であり，果樹も含まれる。

4．生垣の造成

(1)**選択の基本**　前項で記したように，その位置，目的，地域の自然環境などを前提として，好みの樹種を選び，植栽様式を考える。

(2)**樹種の選択**　生垣に適する植物は多いが，その中から特に次のような条件にかない，形態が美しく上品に仕上がる種類が好ましい。

a)性質が強健で枝葉がよく繁茂し，萌芽力に富む適性な種類であること。

b)葉はなるべく小さく枝も細くて，極端に成長が強くないこと。

c)下枝やふところ枝(樹間の小枝)が枯れにくいこと。

d)都市公害に耐え，病害虫が出にくいこと。

e)火気，煙害，強風，積雪などに強いこと。

5．生垣の植え付け

(1)予め植栽地の土を掘り，付近に工事廃材，雑石，笹やヤブガラシなど蔓性の雑草類の根があれば除いておく。

(2)土質が植物の成育に不適であれば，壌土(畑土)と入れ替えておく。また排水も考える。

(3)苗木の倒伏防止のために，四つ目垣か丸太杭に竹(または塩ビ棒)を横に付け，結束しておく。蔓性垣はフェンスなどを設置しておく。

(4)時期は春先の芽が動く前が適期である。

(5)苗は下枝の多いものがよい。

(6)植え付け間隔は苗の高さと枝張り状況によるが，高さが60cm位であれば30cmが基準である。

(7)苗の枝の出方に応じて両傍の苗の枝ぶりとの組み合わせを考え，丁寧に植える。この際，前後に出過ぎた枝や左右で混む枝は，適宜に剪り除く。

(8)土をかけ水を直ぐに与えて支柱に棕櫚縄で結びつけ，根元をよく踏みつける。

(9)大きな苗や木を植えた場合は適当な間隔に丸太を立て，竹などの横押えを渡して，苗を堅固に結束する(布掛け支柱)。また前後の揺れを防ぐために斜めに竹を土中に押し込み，苗の付近で結束する(例：カイズカイブキの列植)。

(10)移植の難しい植物(例：チャ，ピラカンサ，カシ類)は，鉢仕立ての苗を用いれば安全である。

(11)秋まではいずれも水やりに注意すること。

6．生垣の完成まで

(1)枯れ苗が出たら適期に植え直す。

(2)活着苗には5月頃，薄めた油粕の腐汁を与える。また2月頃に遅効性の化成肥料を与える。

(3)植えた初年は徒長枝を切り除き，2年目以後は新梢の2/3～1/3位を2～3芽だけ残して枝配りよく剪る。この際，樹間に透き間ができないように残す芽の位置をきめる。

(4)植物は上長成育が盛んであり，下部の枝よりは上部ほど伸長力が大きいので，上部ほど強剪定が必要である。したがって下方の枝ほど弱く，上方ほど枝数と伸びを止める強い剪定が必要である。

(5)刈り込みの時期は6月の前後と8月末頃の2回以上が望ましい。

(6)目的の高さに達する前には茎はその下部で剪り，枝数と高さもおさえて短く切れば，上端の仕上がりが美しくなる。

(7)樹種による違いはあるが，小苗を植えてから一般的には3～4年で並生垣の高さに達するのが普通である。

7．完成後の管理

　生垣は庭の第1外装であり，その景観美は刈り込みの継続により保たれる。総刈り込み仕立てであれば，上端部，内外面，角部の線と面が整然と仕上げられていると格調も高く品格を見せることになる。列植様式であっても，同じ配慮でそれぞれをほぼ同形同大で刈り込み並べられていてこそ，生垣としての美しさが示される。半自然形，自然形仕立ては適宜な枝の間引き，徒長枝の剪り取りを行い，整姿につとめる。蔓生垣は，伸び過ぎた場合は結束縄をほどき，適宜の長さで剪りつめ，また混み枝を間引き，更新をはかる。

(1)**刈り込み**　あらかじめ竹箒で枝のクモの巣，枯れ葉，ゴミなどを払い落とし，枯れ枝部があれば近くの枝を誘引しておく。

　次に総刈り型であれば，上端部辺りに水糸を張り，刈り込み鋏で水平に切り揃える。次に側面部をまず裏側の中段辺りの部分を横に刈り，次いで上部，下部の順で全体を刈りあげる。表面も同じ順序で行う。そして竹箒で全体を払って枝葉の清掃をする。

(2)**剪定**　生垣は刈り込みだけではなく剪定作業も必要である。混み枝の間引きや切り戻し，太い徒長枝の剪り取りは剪定鋏で行う。

(3)**芯摘み**　針葉樹のカイズカイブキなどは，丁寧に指先でつまんで美しく仕上げる。松類は5～6月に，若枝が葉を伸ばす前に折り取る（みどり摘み）。

(4)**花と実の生垣**は，花芽を育てるために，開花が終わったら直ちに刈り込み，または剪定を行い，蕾の発育を待つ。また，実生垣は花がらを残す。

(5)**施肥**　成育を良くするためには，1～2月の休眠期に寒肥として遅効性の肥料を与える。

(6)**病害**　①ウドンコ病　葉に白くカビが生えるので，冬季に石灰硫黄合剤を与える。窒素質肥料の多用は控える。②赤星病　カイズカイブキとボケ，ナシなどとの間では，この病気が互いに寄主になりやすいので，いずれかの木を近くに植えないようにする。

(7)**虫害**　①アブラムシ　芽先につくことが多い。スミチオンかマラソン乳剤を散布する。②チャドクガ　カンツバキ，ツバキ，チャなどは5～6月と8～9月の年2回，幼虫に葉が食害される。早く発見し，スミチオン乳剤を散布する。他の毛虫類も同様に早く駆除する。③カイガラムシ　幹に着生する成虫には，冬季に機械油乳剤を散布する。このほかに別な病害虫の発生の可能性も考慮し，不明の折には専門家に問い合わせ，対策をすれば安心である。なお諸管理については年間の計画表を作り，事前に手配し，準備と実施をすることが望ましい。

⟨A⟩ Brief History of Hedges

The earliest predecessors of hedges were probably grape vines arranged in rows, still seen in Europe. A painting on the wall of an Egyptian tomb dating from about 1500 B.C. depicts a grape-harvesting scene, with the grape vines lined up neatly.

Excavations of the ancient city of Pompeii, buried in A.D. 79 from an eruption of Mount Vesuvius, revealed upper-class dwellings whose walls contained depictions of gardens with trellises and pergolas covered with vines (Figure 1). Middle-class homes also evidently had rooftop gardens with vine-covered pergolas. Early Rome had professional trimmers who made hedges and practiced topiary, pruning boxwoods and other trees into animal shapes. By the sixteenth and seventeenth centuries, hedges were common in England.

Various fences and hedges are mentioned in classical Japanese literature. The *Kojiki* (Record of Ancient Matters), written in A.D. 712, has a poem about a beautiful Izumo "layered fence" in which the poet wishes to enclose his wife ; we don't know exactly what style or shape of enclosure this refers to. A work entitled *Hitachi Fudoki* (Natural and Cultural History of Hitachi), published in 713, seems to be talking about a hedge in the following description of the property of the Urabe family, who served at Kashima Jingu shrine : "[There is] an inner garden enclosed by a hedge of mountain trees and wild grasses." The *Man'yoshu*, a book of poems collected in about 759, mentions various "fences," including some that are connected with the Shinto religion : woven-reed fence, bamboo fence, shrine fence, *himorogi* (an enclosure of evergreen trees planted to set off a sacred site during a Shinto festival). Two poems by Otomo-no-Yakamochi are of particular interest in tracing the history of hedge use in Japan :

> Is it because people's malicious gossip is as common as the buds on a hedge that I don't see them for days or even months ? (Number 1793)

> I wouldn't languish if only I could catch a glance of my love through the woven bamboo fence in Sae (Number 2530)

Reed fences also appear in *The Tale of Genji* (c. 1000), as do brushwood fences, roofed earthen walls, and trelliswork screens. Sei Shonagon's *Pillowbook* (c. 1002) has a passage that is more clearly about a hedge (albeit untrimmed) : "In the elegant little mountain village there was a wildly growing deutzia hedge with a surprising number of branches sticking out."

A 1697 work by the agriculturist Miyazaki Yasusada entitled *Agricultural Compendium* included descriptions of how to grow seedlings for hedges and three ways of cultivating hedges. Also mentioned were a number of specific plants useful for hedges, including the trifoliate orange, Chinese matrimony vine, aralia, prickly ash, gardenia, mulberry, and fine bamboo. During the Edo period (1603-1867), the authorities in many of Japan's fiefs encouraged the growing of hedges, including those made from Japanese cryptomerias, Japanese cypresses, yews, Japanese privets, evergreen oaks, podocarpuses, pines, trifoliate oranges, Chinese hawthorns, deutzias, aralias, mulberries, Japanese star anises, China laurestines, willows, and bamboo. Aware of the possibility of famine, Uesugi Yozan, lord of the Yonezawa fief, ordered that aralias be planted, since these shrubs can be used for food ; aralia hedges named in honor of him can still be seen today. The thorny trifoliate orange was used throughout Japan as a hedge, but began to disappear in the early twentieth century with the increased import of barbed wire.

Much of Tokyo's urban foliage was destroyed in the Great Kanto Earthquake of 1923, and as the city began spreading into the outskirts thereafter, new varieties of plants and methods of cultivation began to be used. A 1925 study found that there were relatively few hedges in what are now Bunkyo-ku (Bunkyo ward) and Sumida-ku ; these were mainly trifoliate oranges, followed in frequency by sawara cypresses and spindle trees. Many homes in the western suburbs of Suginami and Nakano, in contrast, had hedges, the vast majority of which were sawara cypresses, followed by spindle trees and Chinese hawthorns. (Although not covered in this survey, it is known that from Suginami west, many evergreen oaks were planted as windbreaks.) Most property in Den'en-chofu 3-chome, in the southwest area of Tokyo, had hedges, mainly on top of stone fences and earthen embankments. Other hedges found in the survey were those made from Chinese junipers, azaleas, rose bushes, pyracanthas, camellias, China laurestines, hollies, hiba arborvitaes, sasanquas, chinquapins, ilexes, oleasters, daphnes, Japanese hollies, and andromedas.

A survey of parts of the Osaka suburbs taken the following year found a similar variation in the "density" of hedge planting across different areas, with Chinese pyramid junipers being the most common hedge, followed by Chinese hawthorns, white fragrant olives, and pyracanthas. Other hedges found in the area were made of holm oaks, Japanese privets, evergreen oaks, podocarpuses, sawara cypresses, trifoliate oranges, cryptomerias, rose bushes, spindle trees, Japanese hollies, azaleas, torreyas, Japanese cypresses, and sazanquas. Many were planted on stone fences and earthen embankments.

Much of this greenery was destroyed as a result of the aerial bombings of World War II. At the time, nurseries in Tokyo produced seedlings to distribute to the populace ; I remember selling them at the western entrance of Shinjuku station. Shrubs such as spindle trees were used for hedges, rapidly growing ones reaching about 60 centimeters. During the period of economic reconstruction following the war, wooden houses were built, and trees that went well with the architecture were planted.

Different types of hedges and hedges used for new purposes have appeared in recent years. People tend to move house more, leaving the traditional family home, and new owners or occupants often plant new foliage, such as improved coniferous varieties from abroad, in different ways, such as in boxes. Hedges are also being used increasingly along highways and rail lines.

⟨B⟩ Functions and Uses of Hedges

1. Main Functions
- To enclose a piece of land and protect against trespassing
- To block the view in or out
- To regulate wind, temperature, sunlight, and noise
- To protect against fire, wind, smoke, sand, and the sea
- To purify the air
- To add greenery
- To form borders within a garden

2. Other Uses
- To enjoy new spring greenery, fall colors, flowers, and fruit
- To improve the appearance of or hide concrete structures in gardens
- To prevent garbage from blowing into a garden
- To create a beautiful background, as for an outdoor stage
- Between a street and sidewalk, for safety and greenery
- On roadway medians, to create a sense of safety and

block light from oncoming vehicles
- To set off "borrowed" scenery (i.e., mountains and the like outside the garden used as part of the overall scenery of the garden)
- To create a pictorial image (e.g., a two-layered hedge representing ocean waves)
- For food (e.g., the leaves of the aralia, prickly ash, and Chinese matrimony vine and the fruit of the kumquat)
- To create a maze garden
- To supplement a wall of light blocks (usually vinelike plants)

⟨C⟩ Classification of Hedges

The term "hedges" (in Japanese, *ikegaki*, or "living fence") is used broadly here to include such plants as vines covering concrete walls, as well as in its usual sense of a row of shrubs.

1. By Placement

(1) Exterior hedges
- "Standard" hedges planted directly in the ground, including simple hedgerows
- Short hedges planted in earth atop a stone fence
- Short hedges planted outside a house, wall, etc.
- Hedges planted in plastic or light-concrete boxes, which are placed in plazas, along roads, etc.

(2) Interior/garden hedges
- Hedges planted in gardens, usually short or of medium height, dividing off garden sections, bordering flower beds, hiding concrete structures, etc. Taller hedges form more definitive divisions and can be used to create a maze.
- Hedges as part of rooftop gardens. Consideration must be given to the potential for strong wind.
- Hedges planted in boxes, which may be placed on rooftops, at garden entrances, and on verandas for privacy

2. By Type of Plant
- Hedges made from trees or shrubs, either evergreen or deciduous, with or without flowers or fruit
- Hedges of bamboo or bamboo grass. Varieties with relatively short rhizomes are used, giving a typical Japanese appearance; hedges may be trimmed or left in a partially natural state.
- Hedges of vine plants, which may be woody or herbaceous, evergreen or deciduous. Such vines are usually used with trellises and openwork bamboo fences; some are used to cover concrete walls.
- Thorny hedges, used to prevent entry
- Hedges of flowering and vegetable-bearing plants, often annuals and thus seasonal
- Mixed hedges: hedges of two or more varieties of plants

3. By Shape
- Fully trimmed hedges: hedges trimmed in square or curved shapes; the most common type of exterior hedge.
- Natural hedges: a row of shrubs allowed to grow naturally, without being trimmed into shapes. Some plants grow straight up; others have radiating branches.
- Semi-natural hedges: hedges in various unusual shapes, such as hedgerows of shrubs having branches with round-trimmed ends, and bent-bamboo hedges
- Hedgerows: a row of shrubs with regular spaces between them, each trimmed square, curved, etc.
- Hedges of vine plants (see previous section)

- Fruit tree hedges: Hedgerows of various fruit trees are formed into geometric shapes; for example, the main branches of Asian pear-apple trees are forced to grow straight up, while secondary branches are grown horizontally, diagonally, or vertically. As another example, grape vines may be grown around wires arranged in several horizontal levels.
- Epiphytic hedges: vine plants with aerial roots used to cover concrete walls.

4. By Height
- Tall hedges (more than about 2 meters tall): usually evergreen exterior hedges used mainly as protection from wind. They require scaffolding for pruning and a strip of land on either side.
- Standard-height hedges (about 1.6-2 meters tall): the most common height for a hedge, used mainly to block the line of vision from the outside
- Medium-short hedges: intermediate in height between standard-height and low hedges, used mainly as borders within or around gardens
- Short hedges (less than about 40 centimeters tall): used mainly as edging and atop walls

5. By Optimal Environmental Conditions
Different plants are suited to different environmental conditions. Factors to consider are as follows:

- Temperature: tropical, temperate, cold, and various intermediate temperature zones
- Sunlight: full sun, partial shade, sunny only part of the day
- Moisture level: ranging from dry to damp
- Wind level: Areas with strong winds require plants with strong roots. Not all plants are suited to sea breezes.
- Level of pollution in cities: Additionally, if a hedge is to be used for protection against smoke or spreading fire, an appropriate plant must be chosen.

6. By Plant Element to Be Appreciated
- Leaves (especially fall colors)
- Flowers
- Fruit (decorative or edible)

⟨D⟩ Selecting Plants for a Hedge

The first steps in narrowing down the type of plant or plants you want to use for a hedge are to define the use or purpose of the hedge, decide upon its placement, and ascertain the environmental conditions in which the hedge will be growing. (These factors are described in the previous sections.) Other factors to consider are as follows:

- The plant itself should be a sturdy variety that produces branches and leaves prolifically, but that does not grow overly rapidly.
- Leaves should be small and branches fine.
- Lower branches and inner branches should not dry out easily.
- Plants should be resistant to pest insects, fire, smoke, wind, snow build-up, and, if appropriate, urban pollution.

⟨E⟩ Planting Hedges

The following is a step-by-step guide to planting your hedge:

1. Dig up the area to be planted, removing stones, weeds, roots of vine plants, rubbish, etc.
2. If the soil is poor, replace it with loam. Keep drainage

in mind.

3. To prevent seedlings from falling down, set up a simple fencelike structure, e.g., bamboo or PVC piping attached horizontally to upright wooden stakes. For large seedlings or trees (e.g., Chinese pyramid junipers), the uprights should be sturdy logs planted into the soil at about where the seedlings will be planted. For vines, set up a fence for them to grow on.

4. Plant during the spring, before buds emerge.

5. Select seedlings with a lot of lower branches.

6. The spacing of the plants depends on their height and how much the branches will spread. Plants reaching a height of 0.6 meters should be planted about 0.3 meters apart.

7. Place the seedlings carefully with respect to each other, taking into consideration the positions of existing branches. Trim off branches that extend too far to the front or back or that are already crossing with branches from adjacent seedlings.

8. Fill in the hole with soil and water the seedlings immediately. Secure the seedlings with twine to the fence crossbeams, and press the soil in well. When planting large seedlings or trees, secure the seedlings tightly to the upright logs and bamboo crossbeams; to prevent the whole thing from falling forward or backward, press bamboo poles into the soil at an angle and secure them to the frame near the seedlings.

9. For plants that are difficult to transplant (e.g., tea, pyracantha, oaks), use potted plants.

10. Water the plants sufficiently until the fall.

⟨F⟩ Care Until Hedges Are Fully Grown

· Replace dead seedlings during the next planting season.
· In May, give the seedlings a tea of oil cake suspended in water. The following February, spread slow-acting fertilizer around the plants.
· During the first year following planting, cut off unproductive branches (those that grow overly fast). During the second year and thereafter, trim the hedge back by removing all but two or three buds on from one-third to two-thirds of newly emerged branches. Prune in such a way as to not leave spaces between plants.
· Since growth is more active toward the top of the plant that at the bottom, prune more aggressively at the top.
· Clip twice, around June and late August.
· Before the hedge reaches the desired height, prune the lower part of the stem; keeping the number of branches, as well as the height, down will ensure that the upper part of the hedge has a beautiful appearance.
· Although growth rates vary by plant species, a small seedling will grow to a standard-height hedge in about 3-4 years.

⟨G⟩ Care When Hedges Are Fully Grown

Hedges are the first element of your garden that people will see, so they require continuous care, especially trimming. It is best to make up in advance a yearly schedule of when to perform each of the various aspects of care.

1. Trimming

Prior to trimming, use a broom to remove spider webs, dead leaves, and garbage that might be caught in the hedge. If there are areas of dead branches, try to bend nearby live branches into these areas.

With fully trimmed hedges, the goal is to get the sides, tops, and corners straight and even. For the top of the hedge, stretch a string across at the desired height, making sure the string is perfectly level. Using the string as a guide, clip the hedge at the horizontal using hedge clippers. Do the inside surface next. Divide the hedge (mentally) into upper, middle, and lower thirds. Clip the middle third first, at the perpendicular, moving sideways along the hedge. Do the upper third next, followed by the lower third. Follow this same process for the front surface. Finally, brush the hedge again to clear away stray leaves and twigs.

For hedgerows (noncontiguous plants), try to trim the individual shrubs into the same shape.

2. Pruning

Trimming isn't the only cutting process that a hedge needs. Using pruning shears, cut off overlong, unproductive branches and thin out or cut back dense, tangled branches. These processes are necessary for natural and semi-natural hedges and vines, as well as for hedges that are trimmed. (When pruning vines, untie the cords attaching the vines to the supporting structure.)

The reproductive structures of Chinese pyramid junipers and other conifers should be removed carefully by hand. With pines, do this process in May or June, before the needles on young branches lengthen.

To ensure the developing of flower buds on flowering and fruit plants, cut off flowers as soon as they finish opening.

3. Fertilization

To ensure growth, apply slow-acting fertilizer in January or February, during the dormant season.

4. Preventing Damage from Disease

To prevent mildew from growing on leaves, apply limed sulfur during the winter and avoid overusing fertilizer with a high nitrogen content. To prevent a common condition in which reddish-brown spots form on fruits and leaves, don't plant species that act as hosts for this disease near each other (e.g., Asian pear-apples, roses, Chinese pyramid junipers). Consult with a specialist if your plants should become infected with an unknown blight.

5. Preventing Damage from Insects

Since laws governing the use of insecticides vary from country to country and between jurisdictions within a country, it is best to check with a local nursery or cooperative extension.

高生垣　Tall Hedges

京都・銀閣寺参道のアプローチ　Approach to Ginkaku-ji temple, Kyoto

島根のクロマツの築地松　Japanese black pine, Shimane prefecture

クロマツの築地松（島根県）　L-shaped hedge of Japanese black pine, Shimane prefecture

○京都銀閣寺参道のアプローチ

入口門より本園に至る迄は，上部にヤブツバキを主とする高生垣，下段は粗い石の乱れ積み，その中間は銀閣寺垣の三段構成で高く連なり，道幅が狭くて威圧感がありながら，内部の庭園観賞の期待感を与えてくれる。

○島根の築地松（クロマツ）

宍戸湖の西部の簸川平野では，冬季の北と西からの強風を防ぐために，高さ7～8mのL字型の高生垣が屛風のように所々に見られ，郷土景観にもなっている。

● **Approach to Ginkaku-ji temple, Kyoto**

The narrow approach from the entrance gate to the garden of Kinkaku-ji temple is lined with a three-layered arrangement : a tall hedge of wild-growing camellias at the top, a rough stone wall at the bottom, and a three-tiered Kinkaku-ji fence between them. This imposing structure creates a sense of expectation for what will be seen inside the garden.

● **Japanese black pine (*Pinus thungergii*), Shimane prefecture**

An L-shaped hedge of Japanese black pines, 7-8 meters tall, provides protection from the strong winter winds blowing in from the north and west, on the Hikawa plain, west of Lake Shinji.

イヌマキ（鹿児島県・知覧）　Tall Podocarpus hedge, Chiran, Kagoshima prefecture

シラカシとイヌツゲ　Japanese white oak and Japanese holly (*Ilex crenata*)

○イヌマキ

鹿児島県知覧の高生垣。同地はもと薩摩藩の佐多家の外城跡であり，その武家屋敷はすべてが石垣を積んで囲み，さらにその上部にイヌマキを植えて刈り込み，見事な外廓景観を残して今日に伝えられている。

○シラカシ

北風の強い関東平野に高生垣が風土的景観として多く残されてきている。実生苗を列植し，上部に竹を碁盤目状に張り組んで側枝を誘導結束して仕立てられる。下部はイヌツゲの二段垣。

○イヌツゲ

長さが1.5〜3.0cmの長楕円形の小葉を密生する常緑樹で，生垣仕立て向きであり，陽・陰の両地に向き，刈り込みに耐えて美しい出来栄えを見せるに至る。単にツゲと呼ぶ人もいるが，これとは別種で葉は互生する。

● **Podocarpus (*Podocarpus macrophylla*)**

This tall podocarpus hedge is found in Chiran, Kagoshima, on land that was once the site of the outer castle of the Sata family of the Satsuma fief. The samurai dwelling was entirely surrounded by this trimmed podocarpus hedge atop a stone wall, beautiful even today.

● **Japanese White Oak (*Quercus myrsinaefolia*)**

This variety of oak has long been used as a hedge on the Kanto Plain (around Tokyo), where the north wind is strong. In this example, when the seedlings were planted the top of the plants were woven in a checkerboard pattern with bamboo, and the branches were tied in such a way as to force them to spread well. At the bottom are two tiers of Japanese holly.

● **Japanese holly (*Ilex crenata*)**

The Japanese holly is an evergreen with small, densely growing, oblong leaves 1.5-3 centimeters long. It works well as a hedge, growing in both sunny and shady areas and trimming nicely.

シラカシ（上)とイヌツゲ（下）　Tall hedge of Japanese white oak and Japanese holly

シラカシの内垣　Interior hedge of Japanese white oak

17

シラカシの高生垣（茨城県・土浦市）　Tall hedge of Japanese white oak, Tsuchiura, Ibaraki prefecture

シラカシの高生垣　A tall hedge of Japanese white oak

シラカシとサンゴジュ（埼玉県・鷲宮） Tall hedge of Japanese white oak and Japanese coral tree, Washinomiya, Saitama prefeture

シラカシ（東京都・三鷹市） Japanese white oak, Mitaka, Tokyo

○ **サンゴジュ**

やや水湿地を好み，長さ15cm位の狭長楕円形の葉は肉質であり，防火防風樹として有益で，生垣としての効用が高い。萌芽力があり，枝が密生し，日陰に耐える性質もある。秋に赤く輝く実が付くのでこの名がある。

● **Japanese Coral Tree (*Viburnum awabuki*)**

   Preferring somewhat damp soil, the Japanese coral tree is useful as a wind- and firebreak. It has, narrow oblong leaves 15 centimeters long, grows dense branches, does well in the shade, and produces shiny red fruit in the fall. It is very effective as a hedge.

シラカシの高生垣 Tall Japanese white oak hedge

シラカシの高生垣とイヌツゲの並生垣（茨城県・土浦市） Tall hedge of Japanese white oak and Japanese holly standard-height hedge, Tsuchiura, Ibaraki prefecture

シイの高生垣（東京都台東区・芸術院会館） Tall Chinquapin hedge, The Japan Art Academy, Taito-ku, Tokyo

タチカンツバキの高生垣（千葉県・流山市） Tall winter camellia hedge, Nagareyama, Chiba prefecture

シラカシとモチノキの混ぜ垣（東京都・渋谷区） Japanese white oak and Ilex mixed tall hedge, Shibuya-ku, Tokyo

○タチカンツバキ

カンツバキに近い仲間の立性で勘次郎の名があり，赤い6cm内外の2〜3重の花は12〜2月と長く咲き，耐寒性が強い。6，9月の2回のチャドクガの幼虫に注意すれば，大気汚染，日陰にも耐えて強健に育つ。

● **Winter camellia (*Camellia hiemalis*)**

This is actually a tall relative of the winter camellia, with the variety name Kanjiro. It blooms from December to February with long-lasting double- and triple-blossomed red flowers about 6 centimeters in diameter. Obviously, it is resistant to the cold, as well as to air pollution; it also grows well in the shade. Be careful of certain types of moths in June and September.

シラカシ Japanese white oak

○モチノキ

庭の外周植栽に用いられてきた雌雄別株の常緑樹であり，大気汚染や潮風にも強いが，枝葉が過密し通風日照が悪くなるとスス病が発生し，カイガラムシも多く着生するから，生垣も適度の剪定をする必要がある。

● **Ilex (*Ilex integra*)**

　The ilex is an evergreen dioecious shrub traditionally used to mark the outer boundary of a garden. Though resistant to air pollution and salt air, its densely growing branches and leaves result in poor sunlight penetration and air circulation, leaving the shrub susceptible to sooty mold and scales.

サンゴジュの高生垣（千葉県・流山市）　Tall Japanese coral tree hedge, Nagareyama, Chiba prefecture

モチノキとイヌツゲ　Ilex (*Ilex integra*) and Japanese holly

モチノキ　Ilex

モチノキの高生垣（千葉県・八千代市）　Tall ilex hedge, Yachiyo, Chiba prefecture

21

ヒマラヤスギ（埼玉県花植木センター）　Tall deodar hedge, Saitama Prefecture Garden Plants Center

ヒマラヤスギの高生垣（埼玉県花植木センター）　Tall deodar hedge, Saitama Prefecture Garden Plants Center

ヤマモモ（東京都・世田谷区）　Tall bayberry hedge, Setagaya-ku, Tokyo

○ヒマラヤスギ

大形円錐形で親しまれている針葉樹で，都市公害にも耐性がある。剪定整枝に強く，各種の整形が出来るが，生垣としても枝間が密になり，葉も小形で白緑色の新葉が特に美しく洋風庭園用に好適である。

○ヤマモモ

暖地向きの常緑樹で潮風に強くて海辺地に適し，近年都市部での植栽もふえている。雌雄が別株で6〜7月に2cmほどの球形暗赤色多汁の実を結ぶ果樹でもあり，樹勢が強健で整枝剪定に耐えるので整形も容易である。

○マテバシイ

大気汚染・潮害に強いので近年は都市部での植栽が多いシイの近縁種で，葉は長さが20cm位の長い楕円形で大きくて枝ぶりも粗い。高生垣に向き，防風・防火・防塵などの効果があり，洋風庭園に適している。

○サワラ

ヒノキに似た常緑針葉樹で，葉は薄くて先端はとがる違いが目立つ。刈り込みにより小枝が密生し，葉部は細小できめ細かくて上品な生垣に仕上がる。近年，都市部では減少しているが，和風の生垣として残したいものである。

● Deodar (*Cedrus deodara*)

The deodar is a tall Himalayan cedar in the shape of an elliptical cone. It is resistant to urban pollution and prunes easily into various shapes. Its dense branches make it a good hedge plant, and its small leaves, light green when newly budded, make the plant a nice one for Western-style gardens.

● Bayberry (*Myrica rubra*)

The bayberry is a dioecious evergreen shrub suited to warm climates and, because of its resistance to salt air, to coastal areas; it has become popular in cities in recent years. During June and July it bears dark red, juicy, spherical fruit about 2 centimeters in diameter. A sturdy plant, the bayberry prunes well into shapes appropriate to a hedge.

● *Lithocarpus edulis*

Resistant to air pollution and salt air (as well as wind, fire, and dust), this variety of the chinquapin has become popular in urban areas in recent years. It has an irregular shape overall and oval leaves about 20 centimeters long. It is well suited to Western-style gardens.

● Sawara cypress (*Chamaecyparis pisifera*)

This evergreen conifer resembles the Japanese cypress but has leaves that are thinner and sharper. The fine leaves, as well as the dense branchlets that result from trimming, make for an elegant hedge. The sawara cypress is seen less and less in urban areas, but it is still an excellent plant for a Japanese-style hedge.

マテバシイの高生垣（東京都・小金井市）　Tall *lithocarpus edulis* hedge, Koganei, Tokyo

サワラの高生垣　Tall Sawara cypress hedge

ツバキとマキ（千葉県・流山市）　Camellia and Chinese black pine, Nagareyama, Chiba prefecture

23

カイズカイブキの高生垣（京都市・府立植物園） Tall Chinese pyramid juniper hedge, Kyoto Botanical Garden

○**カイズカイブキ**

イブキの園芸種で，枝は旋回し葉は濃緑色で密生する。戦前は関西で生垣用が多く見られたが，近年は関東地方でも都市公害に強い針葉樹として多用されるに至っている。直線と曲面の二つの仕立て方がある。

● **Chinese pyramid juniper (*Juniperus chinensis* var. *kaizuka*)**
 This conifer, a garden variety of the Chinese juniper, has twisted branches and densely growing dark green leaves. It was popular in hedges in the Kansai region prior to World War II and is now used frequently in the Tokyo area as well for its resistance to urban pollution. It can be trimmed flat or curved.

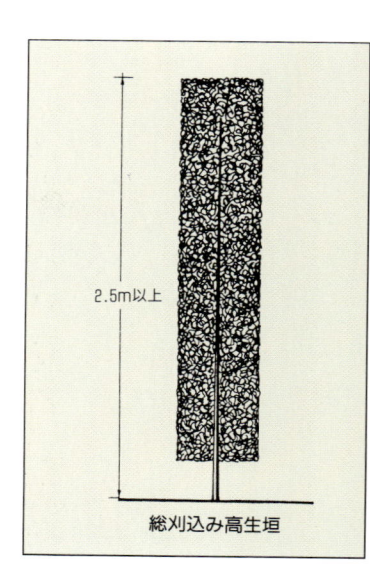

2.5m以上

総刈込み高生垣

カイズカイブキの高生垣 （神奈川県立フラワーセンター大船植物園） Tall Chinese pyramid juniper hedge, Kanagawa Prefectural Ofuna Botanical Garden

カイズカイブキの高生垣 Tall Chinese pyramid juniper hedge

並生垣　Standard-height Hedges

カイズカイブキの並生垣（横浜市・緑区）　Standard-height hedge of Chinese pyramid juniper, Midori-ku, Yokohama

ラカンマキ（千葉県）　Standard-height hedge of Chinese podocarpus, Chiba prefecture

○ラカンマキ

中国原産の常緑性の針葉樹で，日本種のイヌマキに比べて歯の幅が狭く長さも短く，枝先の密生度が美しいので庭木としての利用が多い。潮風に強く，刈り込みが容易で，萌芽力も強い。

○ニッコウヒバ

サワラの変種の小枝は羽毛状に多く付き，葉はより細かくて長く先がとがり，外反するシノブヒバの園芸種で，新葉が特に黄色を呈する。自然形は円錐状であるが，刈り込みに耐えて角型にしても黄色葉を楽しめる。

○イヌマキ

暖地の海辺地に多く見られる常緑針葉樹であり，葉は扁平で長さが10〜15cm，幅0.8〜1.2cmあり，生垣としての利用と共に都市公害に抵抗性が強いことから庭木としても仕立てられ，利用がふえてきている。

○ウバメガシ

葉は5cm内外の長楕円形で固く，若葉は茶褐色であり，姥目樫の名がある。生長は遅いが潮風・都市公害に強く，刈り込みにも耐えて，やや枝葉は粗であるが堅固な生垣が仕立てられる。

○サツキ

ツツジの仲間で開花期が6〜7月と遅い種類であり，園芸品種が多いが，一般的には「大盃」と呼ぶ朱紅色の花を開く品種が多く用いられ，葉はやや茶褐色を呈した葉で落ち着きがあり，庭植えと共に刈り込み向きである。

● **Chinese podocarpus (*Podocarpus chinensis*)**

This native Chinese variety of the podocarpus has leaves shorter and narrower than those of the Japanese variety (*Podocarpus macrophylla*). The branch ends are very dense, making this evergreen coniferous shrub very attractive. It is resistant to salt air and trims well.

● **Nikko cypress (*Chamaecyparis pisifera* var. *plumosa* f.)**

This variety of the sawara cypress has many small featherlike branches with many long, fine, sharp needles that are yellow when they first come out. Left untrimmed, Nikko cypresses are conical; they may be trimmed square, bringing out fresh yellow leaves.

● **Podocarpus (*Podocarpus macrophylla*)**

An evergreen coniferous shrub, the podocarpus is seen frequently in warm coastal regions, and now also in urban areas because of its high resistance to pollution. Its flat leaves measure 10-15 by 0.8-1.2 centimeters.

● **Holm oak (*Quercus phillyraeoides*)**

The holm oak produces oval leaves about 5 centimeters long; the leaves are brown when young. This plant grows slowly but is resistant to salt air and urban pollution. It trims well into a sturdy hedge.

● **Azalea (*Rhododendron indicum*)**

This late-blooming (June-July) variety of azalea has scarlet flowers and small, subdued brown leaves. It can be trimmed or left alone.

サワラの並生垣（東京都・杉並区）　Standard-height hedge of Sawara cypress, Suginami -ku, Tokyo

ニッコウヒバの並生垣（埼玉県・川口市立グリーンセンター）　Standard-height hedge of Nikko cypress(*Chamaecyparis pisifera* var. *plumosa* f.), Kawaguchi Green Center, Saitama prefecture

イヌマキの並生垣（愛知県・明治村）　Standard-height hedge of podocarpus, Meiji-mura, Aichi prefecture

ウバメガシとサツキの並生垣（横浜市・緑区）　Standard-height hedge of Holm oak and Satsuki azalea, Midori-ku, Yokohama

イヌツゲの並生垣（東京都・三鷹市）　Standard-height hedge of Japanese holly, Mitaka, Tokyo

イヌツゲ　Japanese holly

イヌツゲの並生垣　Standard-height hedge of Japanese holly

マメツゲ　Japanese littleleaf ilex

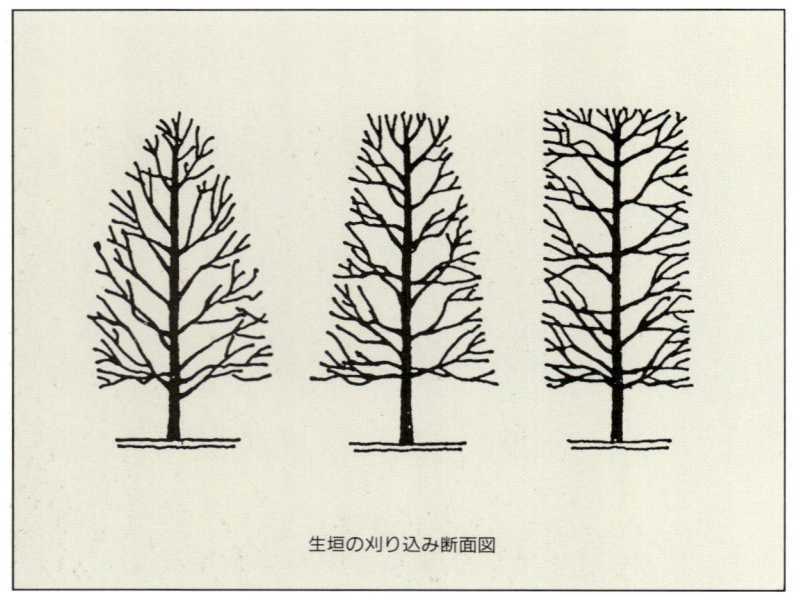

生垣の刈り込み断面図

セイヨウツゲ　Boxwood

○ヒイラギモクセイ

ヒイラギとギンモクセイの雑種とされ，葉は卵状楕円形で長さが8cm内
外あり，先端と縁に粗い刺状の鋸歯をもつ。幹立ちはやや粗大であるが
萌芽力がよく，生垣面の仕上りに強健さが見られる。

● *Osmanthus fortunei*

Osmanthus fortunei is a cross between the holly (*Osmanthus ilicifolius*) and the white fragrant olive (*Osmanthus asiaticus*). It has ovate, serrate leaves about 8 centimeters long. It forms a sturdy hedge with numerous blooms.

ヒイラギモクセイの並生垣（東京都・小金井市）　Standard-height hedge of *Osmanthus fortunei*, Koganei, Tokyo

ヒイラギモクセイの並生垣（東京都・小金井市）　Standard-height hedge of *Osmanthus fortnei*, Koganei, Tokyo

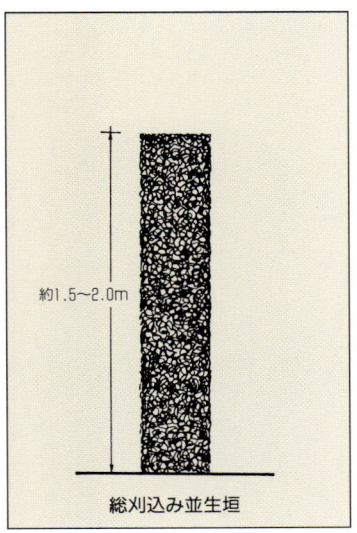

約1.5～2.0m

総刈込み並生垣

ヒイラギモクセイ　*Osmanthus fortunei*

キンモクセイの生垣（東京都・江戸川区・行船公園）Hedge of orange fragrant olive, Gyosen Park, Edogawa-ku, Tokyo

タチカンツバキの並生垣（京都市・大原）Standard-height hedge of winter camellia, Ohara, Kyoto

マサキの並生垣　Standard-height hedge of Spindle tree

キンモクセイの花　Flowers of orange fragrant olive

○**キンモクセイ**
中国原産の秋に橙黄色で香りのよい花を咲かす常緑樹で，生垣としても枝葉が密生するが，幅が広くなるので高生垣向きである。大気汚染には弱くて花を見ないことがあり，また春からの新枝は開花まで切らないでおく必要がある。

○**タチカンツバキ**
高生垣もあるが並生垣に仕立てるのが一般的であり，また年2回のチャドクガの幼虫の発見と駆除のためにも作業がしやすい高さがよい。

○**マサキ**
海岸地に自生する強健な常緑樹で，生垣用を示すマセキ（籬木）が名の由来とする説がマサオキ（真青木）と共にあるという。直立性が強く，生垣用の刈り込み向きであり，緑葉と共に各種の斑入葉種も用いられている。

●**Orange fragrant olive (*Osmanthus fragrans*)**
　This shrub, a native of China, produces fragrant yellow-orange flowers in the fall, as well as densely growing leaves. Because its branches grow out, it can be used in tall hedges. Flowers may not bloom in areas of substantial air pollution. Furthermore, you should wait until after blooming to trim these plants ; otherwise, you may well cut off new bud-producing branches.

●**Tall winter camellia (*Camellia hiemalis*)**
　This plant can be allowed to grow as a tall hedge, but is usually trimmed to a standard-height hedge. The lower height allows for easier removal of moth larvae, which gather on winter camellias twice a year.

●**Spindle tree (*Enonymus japonica*)**
　The spindle tree is a hardy evergreen that flourishes in coastal areas. Growing straight up, it looks good as a trimmed hedge. There are varieties with variegated leaves, as well as the usual plain green ones.

○ベニカナメモチ(レッドロビン)

日本原産のカナメモチと中国原産のオオバカナメモチの雑種で，葉は長楕円形で長さが10cm位あり，春の新葉は紅色が濃くて見映えがし，近年生垣としての需要が多い陽地向きの強健種である。

○カナメモチ

長楕円形で先がとがる5cm余りの硬い葉をもち，新葉は赤味をおびるのでアカメモチともいわれる。晩春に白い小花を開き，晩秋に紅色の実を付けるが，強い刈り込みをすると花と実を見られないのが惜しいことである。

○コトネアスターの刈り込み垣

ベニシタンを含むバラ科の低木の1種であり，本来ならば地上に低生し，枝を四方に広げる樹形であるものを，一般の生垣形に仕立てた形態であり，開花結実すれば赤い実が見られる。

● **Red robin (*Photinia glabra f. red robin*)**

The red robin is a hardy cross between native Japanese and Chinese varieties of the Chinese hawthorn. It has long oblong leaves about 10 centimeters in length that are deep red when they first appear in the spring. The red robin does well in full sun and, judging by the demand for it in recent years, is well suited to hedges.

● **Chinese hawthorn (*Photinia glabra*)**

The Chinese hawthorn has long (5-centimeter) oblong leaves that come to a point ; new leaves are red. The plant produces small white flowers in late spring and red fruit in late fall. Overtrimming can result in loss of fruit production.

● **Cotoneaster (*Cotoneaster*)**

Cotoneasters are low-lying, spreading shrubs useful as ground cover ; they can also be grown into hedges. They bear red fruit.

ベニカナメモチ(レッドロビン)の並生垣（東京都・小金井市） Standard-height hedge of Red robin, Koganei, Tokyo

カナメモチの並生垣　Standard-height hedge of Chinese hawthorn

コトネアスターの並生垣（千葉県・マザー牧場）　Standard-height hedge of Cotoneaster, Mother Farm, Chiba prefecture

キョウチクトウの並生垣（千葉県・東京ディズニーランド）　Standard-height hedge of oleander, Tokyo Disneyland, Chiba prefecture

インド原産の常緑大低木で高さが3～4 mに簇生し，一般にはその自然形のまま列植され，夏季の赤い花を観賞するが，これは花よりは緑葉主体の刈り込み生垣の例であり，利用範囲の多さを示している。

●Oleander (*Nerium oleander*)

Large (3-4 meter-tall) shrubs native to India, oleanders grow in clusters and, when used as hedges, are usually left untrimmed. They are appreciated even more for their greenery than for the red flowers that bloom in the summer. The example shown here is, in fact, trimmed, demonstrating the versatility of this plant.

オオムラサキツツジとヒラドツツジの並生垣　Standard-height hedge of Rhododendron omurasaki and Hirado azalea

サンゴジュの並生垣（皇居）　Standard-height hedge of Japanese coral tree, Imperial Palace, Tokyo

サンゴジュの並生垣（神奈川県立フラワーセンター大船植物園）　Standard-height hedge of Japanese coral tree, Kanagawa Prefectural Ofuna Botanical Garden

○ドウダンツツジ

生垣ほかの刈り込みに強くてよく萌芽し，小枝を密生し，冬の落葉期で
も細かい繁茂ぶりが美しく品が良い。葉も小さくて新緑と秋の紅葉も見
応えがある。また春には小さな壺状の白い花を開き，賑やかに飾ってく
れる。

○ゲッケイジュ

地中海地方原産の常緑樹で雌雄別株，雌の木には赤い実がなる。刈り込
みに強くてやや日陰地でも美しい生垣として仕上がる。また枝葉からよ
い香りを出し，葉は調味香辛料として効用が大きい。

○カラタチ

日本での生垣利用の歴史が古い中国原産の落葉樹で，葉の付け根に3
～6cmの鋭い刺がある。春に白い5弁花，秋に径3cm位の球形の実が黄
色く熟し，北原白秋の「からたちの花」の歌を思い出させる。

● *Enkianthus perulatus*

This shrub produces delicate branches prolifically, so that
when the leaves drop in the fall the plant retains a fine
appearance. The leaves are small, beautiful in both the spring,
when newly emerging, and the fall, when they turn red. Small
white ureceolate (urn-shaped) flowers bloom in the spring, giving
the plant a cheerful appearance. The plant holds up well to
trimming.

● **Laurel (*Laurus nobilis*)**

Native to the Mediterranean region, the laurel is a dioecious
evergreen tree ; the female plants bear red fruit. It trims well as a
hedge and grows beautifully even in partial shade. The leaves
and branches give off a pleasant scent ; the leaves are known for
their versatility in cooking.

● **Trifoliate orange (*Poncirus trifoliata*)**

A deciduous tree native to China, the trifoliate orange has had
a long history of being used as a hedge in Japan. A sharp,
3-6-centimeter-long thorn grows out from the petioles. A white,
five-petaled flower blooms in the spring, and in the fall a round,
light yellow fruit about 3 centimeters in diameter develops.

ドウダンツツジの並生垣　Standard-height hedge of *Enkianthus perulatus*

ゲッケイジュの並生垣　Standard-height hedge of laurel

ゲッケイジュの雄花　Laurel flowers

カラタチの生垣（名古屋市・名城公園）　Trifoliate orange hedge, Meijo Park, Nagoya

中生垣 Medium-Short Hedges

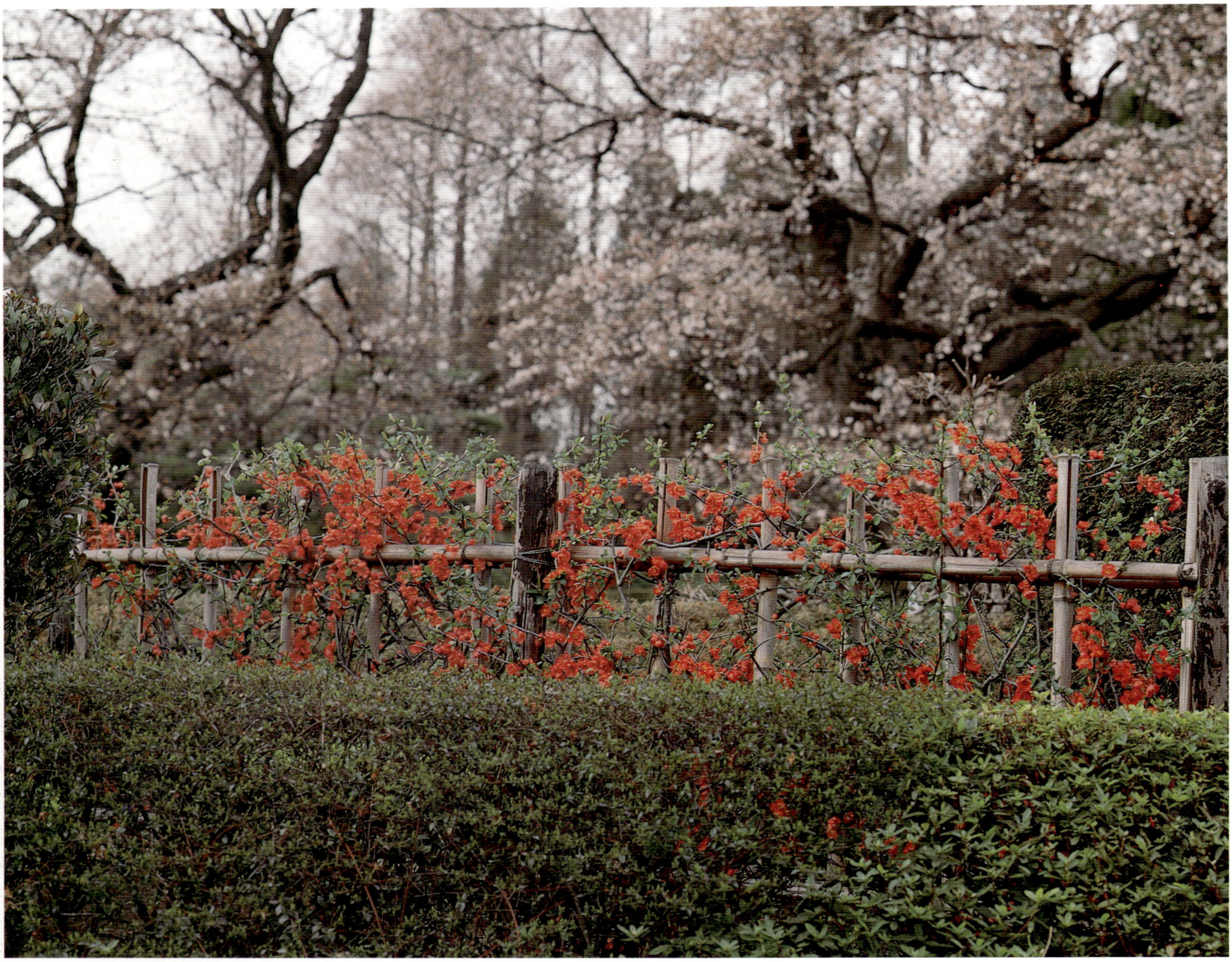

ボケの中生垣（東京都神代植物公園） Japanese quince medium-short hedge, Tokyo Metropolitan Botanical Park

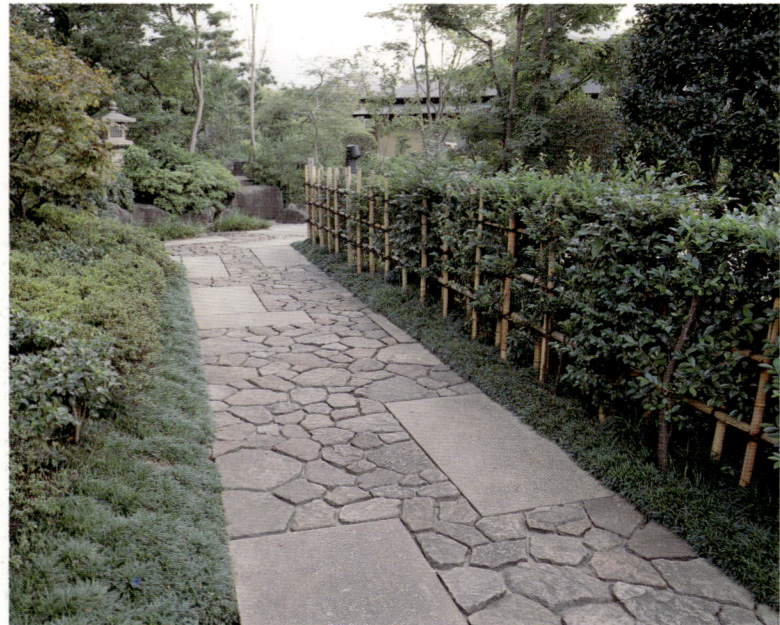

ヒサカキの中生垣（東京都・江戸川区・行船公園） *Eurya japonica* medium-short hedge, Gyosen Park, Edogawa-ku, Tokyo

○**ボケ**

高さ2 m余になる中国原産の落葉性の花木で，春に白・赤の径3 cm位の花を開き，園芸品種もある。枝には刺があるが，枝の乱れを防ぐために秋に花芽を見ながら強剪定をすれば，美しい花生垣を楽しむことができる。

○**ヒサカキ**

サカキのように神前に供されてきた日本産の強健種で，葉はより小さくて鋸歯があり，半陰地を好む。剪定に強くて多くの枝葉を密生することから刈り込み向きであり，日当りの少ない場所の生垣として適する。

● **Japanese quince (*Chaenomeles lagenaria*)**

This deciduous tree is native to China and grows up to 2 meters tall. Its white and red flowers, about 3 centimeters in diameter, bloom in the spring. To prevent overgrowth of the thorny branches and produce a flowery hedge, prune well in the autumn, taking care not to cut off branches with flower buds.

● ***Eurya japonica***

Native to Japan, this hardy plant is often presented as an offering at Shinto shrines. Its leaves are serrate ; they and the branches grow densely. The plant trims well as a hedge and prefers partially shaded areas.

イヌツゲとキャラボクの中生垣（横浜市・あざみ野）　Medium-short hedge of Japanese holly and Japanese yew, Azamino, Yokohama

○キャラボク

日本庭園の景観樹として各様の刈り込み仕立てをされていて面白い樹形のものが見られ，また玉仕立て品は列植，点植，境栽植えにされている。大気汚染に強く陰陽の両地に耐え，乾燥に強い。

○アベリア

ハナツクバネウツギなどの日本名もあるが，一般に学名のこの名で呼ばれる半常緑性の中国原産の改良園芸植物で，一般には放射状に立つ姿の自然形仕立てが多いが，刈り込み作りもなされ，7〜11月に白花を群生する。

● **Japanese yew (*Taxus cuspidata var. umbraculifera*)**

The Japanese yew lends itself well to being trimmed into various interesting shapes, seen often in traditional Japanese gardens. Hedgerows and borders of hemispherically trimmed Japanese yews are common. The plant does well in both sun and shade, and stands up well to pollution and drought.

● **Abelia (*Abelia grandiflora*)**

This is an improved garden variety of a semi-evergreen plant native to China. Bunches of white flowers bloom from June to November. Its diagonal-pointing branches are usually left natural, but the plant can be trimmed as well.

アベリアの中生垣　Abelia(*Abelia grandiflora*) medium-short hedge

35

テイカカズラの生垣（東京都・北区・旧古河庭園） Climbing bagbane (*Trachelospermum asiaticum*) hedge, former Koga Garden, Kita-ku, Tokyo

アズマネザサの生垣（横浜市・三渓園） Ground bamboo grass hedge, Sankeien Garden, Yokohama

○テイカカズラ

東京都北区にある旧古河庭園の本館前には洋風庭園があり，西洋バラや
ツツジ類が植えられている。そして登り斜面の階段の両側は境栽生垣と
してテイカカズラが低く刈り込まれている。

○アズマネザサ

関東・東北地方に広く群生する笹の1種の害草ではあるが，庭園で地被
用として低く平面に刈り込みもされている。写真は，低生垣仕立てをし
ている例であり，強健であるために強い茎刈りが行われている。

○トキワサンザシ

ピラカンサの1種。葉は狭倒卵形で幅が広く，枝には刺がある南欧・西
アジア原産の常緑樹で，秋から初冬にかけての鮮紅色の実が美しい。刈
り込みに強く耐寒性があり，欧州で多く植栽され，数品種がある。

● **Climbing bagbane (*Trachelospermum asiaticum*)**
A stairway in a park in Kita-ku, Tokyo, is lined with a low
hedge of this plant. (See "Vine Hedges," below, for a fuller
description of this plant.)

● **Ground bamboo grass (*Pleioblastus chino* Makino)**
This variety of bamboo grass (sasa) is considered a weed in the
Tokyo region and north, where it grows abundantly. Shown here
is a short hedge of ground bamboo. Its stalks trim well.

● **Pyracantha (*Pyracantha coccinea*)**
The pyracantha is a plant native to southern Europe and
western Asia with wide ovate leaves and thorns ; this variety
bears beautiful scarlet fruit from the fall to early winter. It does
well as a trimmed hedge and is resistant to cold. Numerous
varieties are cultivated in Europe.

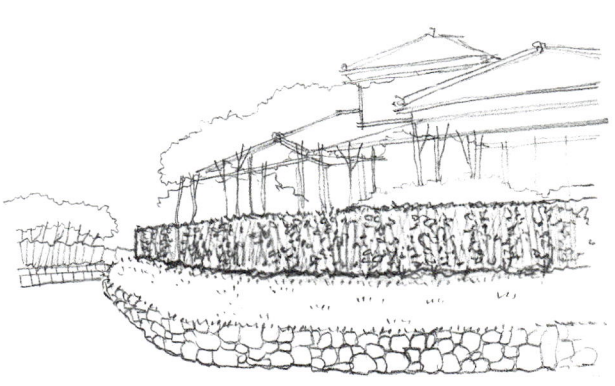

トキワサンザシ（ピラカンサ）の生垣（東京都・新宿区）　Pyracantha hedge, Shinjuku-ku,
Tokyo

トキワサンザシ（ピラカンサ）の中生垣（埼玉県・浦和市植物園）　Pyracantha medium-
short hedge, Urawa Botanical Garden, Saitama prefecture

ヒマラヤピラカンサの実　Himalayan Pyracantha barries

イヌマキの中生垣（愛知県・明治村）　Medium-short hedge of Podocarpus, Meiji-mura, Aichi prefecture

○ナワシログミ

水田の苗代をつくる頃の初夏に実が熟すことからこの名がある常緑の低木で，枝は硬くて針になるものが多く，葉は長さ5㎝ほどの長楕円形で，やはり硬く，裏表には銀白色の鱗片が付いている。

● **Silverthorn (_Elaeagnus pungens_)**

The silverthorn is a shrub that bears fruit in early summer when rice seedlings are coming up in the paddies. It has hard branches with numerous needles and hard oblong leaves about 5 centimeters long, with silver scales.

ナワシログミの中生垣（愛知県・緑化センター）　Silverthorn medium-short hedge, Green Center, Aichi prefecture

チャの生垣（京都市・大原）　Tea hedge, Ohara, Kyoto

○チャ

製茶用の常緑樹で，その生産地では手摘み用の低い列植風景が見られるが，生垣としても刈り込みに強く，枝葉が密生し，和趣味向きの雅致ある外垣・内垣が喜ばれる。秋が深まってから白い花を下向きに咲かせる。蕾も愛らしい。

● Tea (*Thea sinensis*)

When these evergreen shrubs are cultivated for their beverage-producing leaves, they are kept short and separated from one another for easy hand-picking. When used for hedges, however, they trim well and create an elegant Japanese appearance whether in the front or back garden. Drooping white flowers bloom in the fall.

チャの中生垣　Tea medium-short hedge

サツキの中生垣（京都市・大原）Satsuki azalea medium-short hedge, Ohara, Kyoto

ヒイラギモクセイの中生垣（東京都・世田谷区・砧公園）*Osmanthus fortunei* medium-short hedge, Kinuta Park, Setagaya-ku, Tokyo

アラカシの中生垣（愛知県・緑化センター）Ring-cupped oak medium-short hedge, Green center, Aichi prefecture

○アラカシ

関東地方のシラカシと共に関西では生垣として多く使われ，葉は楕円～長楕円形で縁に粗い鋸歯がある。強い剪定に耐えて枝葉を密生し，和趣味の庭に向いて味わい深さがある。低・高の生垣にも利用される。

○ツバキ

日本原産の常緑樹でヤブツバキ，ユキツバキの両種とそれからの品種が多い代表的な花木である。開花期や花の色の違いがあるが性質は強健であり，生垣として品種を並べて花を観賞する楽しみ方もできる。

● *Ring-cupped oak (Quercus glauca)*

This variety of oak is popular in hedges in the Kansai (Osaka-Kyoto) region. It has oval or oblong serrate leaves that grow densely, as do the branches. The plant stands up well to pruning, making it good for hedges, either tall or short.

● **Camellia (*Camellia japonica*)**

Flowering trees native to Japan, camellias are now available in numerous varieties. Although they differ in terms of flowering period and flower color, all are hardy. A row of several varieties makes for a beautiful and interesting hedge.

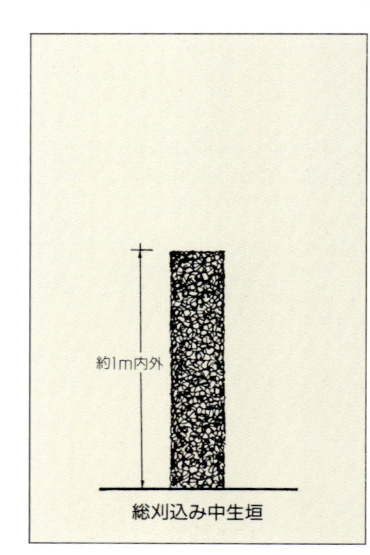

約1m内外

総刈込み中生垣

ツバキの中生垣　Camellia medium-short hedge

ツバキの中生垣（京都市・大原）Camellia medium-short hedge, Ohara, Kyoto

41

ドウダンツツジの中生垣　*Enkianthus perulatus* medium-short hedge

キャラボクの生垣（神奈川県・伊勢原）Japanese yew hedge, Isehara, Kanagawa prefecture

ニッコウヒバの生垣（埼玉県・鷲宮）　Nikko cypress hedge, Washinomiya,
Saitama prefecture

ヒサカキの中生垣（東京都・江戸川区・行船公園）　*Eurya japonica* medium-short hedge,
Gyosen Park, Edogawa-ku, Tokyo

マキの生垣　Chinese black pine hedge

低生垣　Short Hedges

キャラボク（左）とセイヨウツゲ（右）の生垣（横浜市・こども植物園）　Hedges of Japanese yew, left, and boxwood, right, Children's Botanical Garden, Yokohama

○セイヨウツゲ

日本原産のツゲに代わる主役的存在であり、品種数も多い。近年は日本でも多く植えられ、特に新緑の美しさが喜ばれ、冬には褐変する。春に出るツゲノメイガの幼虫の食害が要注意である。

○ハクチョウゲ

葉の長さは2cmほどの狭長楕円形、枝も細くて密生する半常緑性で、強い刈り込みに耐えて萌芽力がよいことから、高さ20〜30cm位の花壇の囲い生垣ほかの利用もある。初夏に径1cmほどの5裂の白い花をつける。

● **Boxwood (*Buxus sempervirens* spp.)**

   This is one of the many varieties of the boxwood native to Japan. It is appreciated in Japan for its new green leaves in the spring, which turn brown in the winter. Beware of a characteristic moth that attacks the tree in the spring.

● *Serissa japonica*

   This semi-evergreen shrub has fine, dense branches and narrow oblong leaves about 2 centimeters long. Prolific, it trims well as a hedge and is useful as a border for flower boxes; it grows to a height of 20-30 centimeters. In early summer it blooms with five-lobed white flowers about 1 centimeter in diameter.

ハクチョウゲの低生垣（東京都・墨田区・清澄庭園）　*Serissa japonica* short hedge, Kiyozumi Garden, Sumida-ku, Tokyo

マメツゲ（マメイヌツゲ）の低生垣（皇居）　Japanese littleleaf ilex short hedge, Imperial Palace, Tokyo

マメツゲの低生垣（皇居）　Japanese littleleaf ilex short hedge, Imperial Palace, Tokyo

セイヨウツゲの低生垣（千葉県・東京ディズニーランド）Boxwood short hedge, Tokyo Disneyland, Chiba prefecture

約40cm内外

総刈込み低生垣

オウゴンタマイブキの低生垣（埼玉県・川口市立グリーンセンター）　Chinese juniper short hedge, Kawaguchi Green Center, Saitama prefecture

ドウダンツツジの低生垣（栃木県・古峰神社・古峰園）　White enkianthus perulatus short hedge, Kohoen Garden, Tochigi prefecture

キャラボク（東京都神代植物公園）　Japanese yew, Tokyo Metropolitan Jindai Botanical Park

○オウゴンタマイブキ

「伊吹」は常緑の高く育つ針葉樹であり，その枝を挿し木して低く半球状に育てたのを「玉伊吹」と呼び，葉が黄色い品種がこれである。緑葉樹と共に列植すると美しいが，雪には弱いので，あらかじめ縄で縛って枝折れを防ぐ必要がある。

○キャラボク

寒地ではイチイの生垣が多いが，その変種で葉が螺旋状に多くつく低木であり，刈り込みに強くて生垣や各様の形に仕立てられている。樹勢が強く陰陽，乾湿の両地でよく生育をする。

○カンツバキ

這い性の低花木で，12〜2月まで径6cm内外で3〜5重の紅色の花を開く「獅子頭」で，低木としての利用が多いが，また中生垣作りをして二段生垣の下段植えや，写真のような仕切り植栽にも適している。

○マメツゲ（マメイヌツゲ）

イヌツゲの変種。葉が1〜1.5cmの半球形に上面がふくらみ，豆状になるのでこの名がある。一般に径が30〜60cmの半球状に仕立てられ，土坡上に列植される例が多い。放置するとイヌツゲ状の葉に戻る。

● **Chinese juniper shrub (*Juniperus chinensis*)**

The Chinese juniper is a tall evergreen tree. In this case, cuttings have been planted and trimmed into a short hemispheres. Planting Chinese juniper shrubs in rows with evergreen trees results in a beautiful arrangement, but secure the shrubs with rope, as they are not resistant to snow piled on them.

● **Japanese yew (*Taxus cuspidata var. umbraculifera*)**

This shrub, a variety of the yew, produces numerous spirally arranged leaves. Holding up well to trimming, it is cut into a variety of shapes. The plant does well in both sun and shade, and stands up well to drought.

● **Winter camellia (*Camellia hiemalis*)**

This low-lying, creeping shrub blooms with three- to five-layered crimson flowers from December to February. It works well as a medium-short or two-tiered hedge.

● **Japanese littleleaf ilex (*Ilex crenata var.*)**

This variety of the Japanese holly has bean-shaped leaves 1-1.5 centimeters long. The overall plant usually has a semicircular shape and grows to a height of 30-60 centimeters. It is usually planted in hedgerows atop stone walls. The leaves "return" to the oblong shape of the regular Japanese holly if the plant is not trimmed regularly.

オウゴンキャラボクの低生垣きの縁植え（札幌市・百合ケ原公園）Apron hedge of Japanese yew, Yurigahara Park, Sapporo

セイヨウウツゲの低生垣（東京都・港区）Apron hedge of Boxwood short hedge, Minato-ku, Tokyo

ツツジの低生垣の縁植え（東京都・立川市・昭和公園）Apron hedge of Azalea, Showa Park, Tachikawa, Tokyo

ベニカナメモチ（レッドロビン）の生垣　Red robin hedge

カンツバキの低生垣（皇居）Winter camellia short hedge, Imperial Palace, Tokyo

マメツゲの低生垣の縁植え（東京都神代植物公園）Apron hedge of Japanese littleleaf ilex, Tokyo Metropolitan Jindai Botanical Park

蔓生垣 Vine Hedges

ツルバラ(神奈川県・小田急向が丘遊園) Climbing rose, Odakyu Mukogaoka Amusement Park, Kanagawa prefecture

○ ツルバラ

西洋バラの中で蔓性種は系統と品種数が多く，また着花数も豊富であり，バラ園ではスクリーン，フェンス，ポール，アーチ，トンネル，ベンチなどと様々な仕立て方をする。また家庭では外垣作りが多い。

● Climbing rose (*Rosa* spp.)

There are numerous classifications and varieties of viny roses, most of which bear flowers prolifically. They are seen in rose gardens on screens, fences, arches, poles, tunnels, benches, and other structures. In residential gardens they can be used in the creation of exterior hedges.

ツルバラの生垣(東京都神代植物公園) Climbing rose hedge, Tokyo Metropolitan Jindai Botanical Park

○**ナニワイバラ**
台湾・中国原産の常緑性の蔓状低木で，茎には刺があり，長く伸びる。
葉は３出複葉で光沢があり，春には小枝の先に径５〜９cmの白色の香り
のよい５弁花が１個ずつ開く。難波とは，おそらく大阪の植木屋が広め
たための名であろう。

○**モッコウバラ**
中国原産の半常緑性の蔓状バラで，枝を４mほどに長く伸ばすが，刺の
ないのが特徴である。５月頃に白または淡黄色で径2.5cmほどの八重咲き
の花を付ける。香りのよいのは白色花の方である。

○**ツキヌキニンドウ**
北米原産の半常緑蔓性低木で，花に近い葉は対生する２枚が合着してい
て，その先に花穂が付くのでこの名がある。強健種であり，５〜10月の
間に休まず蔓の先に黄赤色の筒状の花を咲き続ける。

● **Cherokee rose (*Rosa laevigata*)**
　The Cherokee rose, actually native to China and Taiwan, is a
thorny, vinelike evergreen climbing shrub with lustrous ternate
leaves. A single fragrant, five-petaled white flower 5-9
centimeters in diameter buds from the tip of each branchlet.

● *Rosa banksiae*
　This semi-evergreen thornless viny rose is native to China and
has branches growing up to 4 meters long. In May it blooms with
white or light yellow double-blossomed flowers 2.5 centimeters in
diameter. The white flowers have a nicer fragrance than do the
yellow.

● **Coral honeysuckle (*Lonicera sempervirens*)**
　This semi-evergreen vine shrub is native to North America. It
is a hardy plant, producing yellow tubular flowers at the tip of
the tendrils from May to October.

ナニワイバラの生垣（東京都・世田谷区）　Cherokee rose hedge, Setagaya-ku, Tokyo

モッコウイバラの生垣　*Rosa banksiae* hedge

ツキヌキニンドウの生垣　Coral honeysuckle hedge

トケイソウの蔓生垣　Passionflower vine hedge

トケイソウの花　Passionflower flowers

トケイソウの蔓生垣　Passionflower vine hedge

○トケイソウ

ペルー，ブラジル原産の常緑蔓性低木で，葉は掌状に5〜7深裂し互生して付き，夏から秋にかけて7〜10cmの花弁，萼片各5枚が同大の一見時計盤に似た花を付け，のち長さ5cm位の卵形の実を結ぶ。

● Passionflower (*Passiflora coerulea*)

　The passionflower is an evergreen vine shrub native to Brazil and Peru with alternating five- to seven-lobed palmate leaves. From summer to fall it produces flowers with five petals and five sepals, each 7-10 centimeters long ; subsequently, ovate fruit about 5 centimeters long is produced.

ムベの蔓生垣　*Stauntonia hexophylla* vine hedge

ムベの実　*Stauntonia hexophylla* fruits

ムベの花　*Stauntonia hexophylla* flowers

○ムベ

アケビに似ていて常緑性であるためにトキワアケビとも呼ばれ，葉も大きく3～7枚の掌状複葉であり，茎は他物に巻き付いて伸長する。4月下旬に紫色を帯びた白色花を開き，夏から実を結んで晩秋に紫色に熟する。

● *Stauntonia hexophylla*

This evergreen plant has large five- to seven-lobed palmate compound leaves, and stems that wind around other objects as they grow. In late April, the vine blooms with white-and-purple flowers ; fruit appears in the summer and turns purple in late fall.

ノウゼンカズラの蔓生垣　Trampet creeper vine hedge

ノウゼンカズラの花　Trumpet creeper flowers

カロライナジャスミンの蔓生垣（東京都・新宿区・戸山公園）　Yellow jessamine vin hedge, Toyama park, Shinjuku-ku, Tokyo

フウセンカズラの蔓生垣　Ballon vine hedge

○**ノウゼンカズラ**
中国原産の落葉蔓性木本で，茎から気根を出して這い上り，葉は奇数羽状複葉で対生，夏に赤黄色で7cm内外の筒状花を咲き続ける。よく似たアメリカノウゼンカズラは橙紅色花を開き，花茎は3～4cmである。
○**カロライナジャスミン**
北米南部から中央アメリカに分布する半常緑性の蔓植物で，カロライナはアメリカの州名である。寒さには弱いが比較的に強健で蔓を長く伸ばし，初夏に黄色い花を次々と咲かせる。生垣，棚づくりによい。

● **Trumpet creeper (*Campsis chinensis*)**
　This variety of the trumpet creeper is a deciduous woody vine native to China that produces odd-pinnate compound leaves, aerial roots from its stalk as it climbs upward, and, during the summer, orange tubular flowers about 7 centimeters long. The American variety of the trumpet creeper (*Campsis radicans*), which closely resembles the one shown here, has deep-red-orange flowers with stalks 3-4 centimeters long.
● **Yellow jessamine (*Gelsemium sempervirens*)**
　The yellow jessamine (or yellow jasmine) is a semi-evergreen vine distributed from the southern United States to Central America. It is sturdy and grows long, lending itself well to a trellis hedge, but succumbs easily to the cold. It produces yellow flowers in early summer.

○テイカカズラ

本州の秋田県以南に自生する常緑性の蔓低木で，茎は長さが10mにも達するほど伸びる強健さがあり，巻き付いたり気根を出して他物に着生する。初夏の頃，径2㎝ほどの白花を開き，芳香を放つ。フェンスに絡ませたりポール仕立てがされている。

● **Climbing bagbane (*Trachelospermum asiaticum*)**

This evergreen vine shrub grows wildly from Akita pretecture on south. Its hardy stalks, reaching lengths of 10 meters, wind around objects (poles and fences are often used) as they grow and produce aerial roots. Fragrant white flowers about 2 centimeters in diameter bloom in the early summer.

ビナンカズラの蔓生垣　*Kazura japonica* vine hedg

ビナンカズラの花　Flowers of *Kazura japonica*

テイカカズラの蔓生垣　Climbing bagbane (*Trachelospermum asiaticum*) vine hedge

ビナンカズラの実　Berries of *Kazura japonica*

桂離宮の腰折れ垣　Bent-bamboo hedge, Katsura Imperial Villa, Kyoto

セイヨウバクチノキの縁植え生垣　Apron hedge of cherry laurel

○ **桂離宮の腰折れ垣**
桂川に沿う道の外垣は，園内のハチクの先端を折り曲げ，およそ２ｍほどの高さで杭や板，竹などで押さえ，長さ250ｍばかりが連なる生垣である。その山荘風の素朴さを味わいながら北上すると桂垣に変り，御成門に達する。

○ **セイヨウバクチノキ**
東欧，小アジア原産の常緑樹で葉は硬く，暗緑色の大きな長楕円形で，４月に長い穂に白い小花を咲かせる。萌芽力が強く刈り込みに耐えてよく育つが，やや湿度のある土地を好む。

● **Bent-bamboo hedge at Katsura Imperial Villa**
The road along the Katsura River in Kyoto is lined for about 250 meters with a bent-bamboo hedge, which is made by bending hachiku bamboo (a very dark green variety) with stakes and bamboo pieces to give a final height of 2 meters. The hedge eventually turns into a Katsura bamboo-branch fence, which ends in the gate to the villa.

● **Cherry laurel (*Prunus laurocerasus*)**
Native to eastern Europe and Asia Minor, this evergreen tree has large, oblong, dark green, brittle leaves. Small white flowers bloom on spikes during April. The plant stands up very well to trimming and prefers slightly moist soil.

カイズカイブキの生垣　Chinese pyramid juniper semi-natural hedge

カイズカイブキの玉散らし生垣（横浜市・緑区）　Chinese pyramid juniper hedge, Midori-ku, Yokohama

カイズカイブキの土坡垣　Chinese pyramid juniper hedge on a stone fence

カイズカイブキの列植生垣（千葉県・マザー牧場）　Chinese pyramid juniper hedgerows, Mother Farm, Chiba prefecture

○**カイズカイブキ**
生垣仕立ての外面は直線状が普通であるが、本種のように側枝が巻き込み独特の螺旋模様を呈するために、その外観を見せるための半自然形作りの生垣も多く見られる。

○**ナリヒラダケ**
本州中南部，四国，九州の原産で高さが5〜7mに直立し，節間と枝が短く，節から3〜5本が叢生し，緑が美しいので家庭用の観賞や目隠しとして多く植えられている。大名竹の名もあり，冬の寒風にも強い。

● **Chinese pyramid juniper (*Juniperus chinensis* var. *kaizuka*)**
The exterior surface of a Chinese pyramid juniper hedge is usually trimmed flat. The variety shown here, however, features lateral branches that grow in spiral patterns, making it appropriate for a semi-natural hedge.

● **Narihira bamboo (*Semiarundiaria fastuosa*)**
Native to central and southern Honshu, Kyushu, and Shikoku islands, this variety of bamboo grows to heights of 5—7 meters and has closely spaced nodes and short branches. Three to five branches grow out of the nodes, resulting in a beautiful green plant well suited to gardens and screening purposes. It withstands cold winter winds well.

カイズカイブキの列植生垣　Chinese pyramid juniper hedgerows

ナリヒラダケの生垣（横浜市・緑区）　Narihira bamboo hedge, Midori-ku, Yokohama

ミヤギノハギの自然形生垣(東京都・墨田区・向島百花園)　Natural hedge of Japanese purples, Mukojima Hyakkaen, Sumida-ku, Tokyo

洋種レンギョウの自然形生垣(東京都・立川市・国営昭和記念公園)　Weeping golden bell natural hedge, Showa Kinen Park, Tachikawa, Tokyo

○ミヤギノハギ

ハギの仲間では葉が狭長で枝も長く伸びて最も優美な姿を示し、紫紅色の花を7月頃から咲かせる。根元から多く伸びる枝を刈り込まないで列植する生垣は原始風ではあるが、四つ目垣が支持をしている。

○ナンテン

難を転じるという意味付けをし、また秋からの赤い実を賞するためもあって、庭植えにされてきている立ち性の常緑低木で、若枝を次々に立てながら生育する強健種である。花は梅雨頃に白い小花を付け、紅葉美も楽しめる。

● *Japanese purple (Lespedega penduliflora)*

This is a relative of the bush clover, with long, narrow leaves, numerous long branches growing up from the base of the plant, deep crimson flowers that bloom in July, and a beautiful shape overall. Although these plants are ordinarily arranged into hedgerows and left untrimmed, the one shown here is supported by a four-eyed bamboo fence.

● **Heavenly bamboo (*Nandina domestica* Thumb.)**

The nandin is a sturdy upright evergreen shrub that produces new branches prolifically. Small white flowers bloom in the rainy season (early summer), and red fruit is produced in the fall. The leaves turn red in the fall as well.

ナンテンの自然形生垣（埼玉県・森林公園）　Hevenly bamboo natural hedge, Forest park, Saitama prefecture

カンチクの自然形生垣（東京都・小金井市）　Marbled bamboo natural hedge, Koganei, Tokyo

オウゴンコノテガシワの列植　Arborvitae hedgerow

○ **オウゴンコノテガシワ**

中国原産の常緑針葉低木で，各枝は直立し葉は扁平になり，表裏が見分けにくいことから「児の手」の名がある。1株ずつを列植し観賞する洋風庭園向きであり，本種のような黄葉品は庭に明るさを増してくれる。

● **Arborvitae (_Thuja occidentalis_)**

An evergreen coniferous shrub native to China, the arborvitae looks good in hedgerows in Western-style gardens. The variety here, with its yellow leaves, adds brightness to a garden.

オウゴンコノテガシワの列植　Arborvitae hedgerow

コノテガシワの列植（東京都庁前）　Hedgerow of Chinese arborvitae, Tokyo Metropolitan Goverment Office

オウゴンイトヒバの列植（埼玉県・川口市立グリーンセンター）　Hedgerow of golden hiba arborvitae, Kawaguchi Green Center, Saitama prefecture

ニオイヒバ（下）とハイビャクシン（上）の列植（神奈川県立フラワーセンター大船植物園）
Hedgerows of *Thuja occidentalis* Linn., below, and Creeping Japanese janiper, above, Kanagawa prefectural Ofuna Botanical Garden, Kanagawa prefecture

ヒラドツツジの列植　Hedgerow of Hirado azalea

ヒラドツツジの列植生垣（皇居）　Hedgerow of Hirado azalea, Imperial Palace, Tokyo

○ヒラドツツジ

長崎県平戸で古くから栽培されてきた大形のツツジの1群の名であり，品種数が多く，花径は10cm余りのもの，花色が紫・藤・朱・とき・紅・桃・白などと多様であり，排気ガス・煤煙にも耐える強健種である。

○ヒイラギナンテン

葉は羽状複葉で硬く，縁に刺があり，葉並びが南天に似ているのでこの名がある常緑低木。春に黄色い小花を穂につけて下がり咲く。茎は分岐して多く，特に刈り込まない自然形で玄関前や別に列植，密植をする。

● **Hirado azalea (*Rhododendron weyrichii* X)**

　　The name hirado azalea refers to the numerous large varieties of azalea long grown in the Hirado region of Nagasaki prefecture. There are more than ten types of flower stalks, and flowers of purple, lavender, vermilion, crimson, pink, white, and other shades. The plants are resistant to exhaust fumes and soot.

● **Japanese mahonia (*Mahonia japonica*)**

　　This evergreen shrub has compound pinnate leaves edged with thorns. In the spring, small yellow flowers bloom from spikes and hang down. The plant's stalks branch out prolifically, making the shrub appropriate for hedgerows and around house entrances, in either case untrimmed.

ヒイラギナンテンの列植　Hedgerow of Japanese mahonia

ヒイラギナンテンの列植（名古屋市・緑化センター）　Hedgerow of Japanese mahonia, Green Center, Nagoya

ヒラドツツジの列植　Hedgerow of Hirado azalea

オウゴンクジャクヒバの列植（京都府立植物園） Hedgerow of Golden peacock hiba, Kyoto Botanical Garden

ゴールドクレストの列植　Hedgerow of Goldcrest

アツバキミガヨランの列植　Hedgerow of Spanish dagger

メキシコからカリフォルニアにかけて原産するヒノキ科のイトスギの仲間の園芸品種であり，枝先に細くて短い針葉が密生し若葉は明るい黄緑色で美しい。生垣風の列植，鉢に植えて観葉植物にされる。

● **Gold crest**

   This is a garden variety of the cypress that made its way to Japan from Mexico by way of California. Fine, short, bright yellow needles grow densely from the ends of the branches. Gold crests can be planted as hedgerows, or in pots as ornamentals.

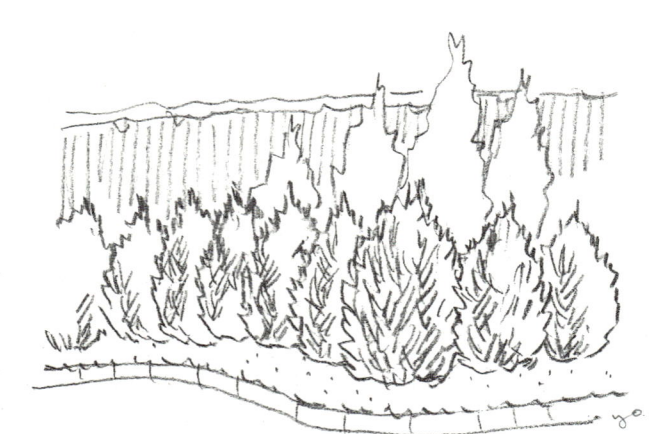

カイズカイブキの列植　Hedgerow of Chinese pyramid juniper

カイズカイブキの列植　Hedgerow of Chinese pyramid juniper

カイズカイブキの列植（千葉県・八千代市）　Hedgerow of Chinese pyramid juniper, Yachiyo, Chiba prefecture

タマイブキの列植（埼玉県・袋田） Hedgerow of Chinese juniper shrub, Fukuroda, Saitama prefecture

タマイブキの列植（愛知県・明治村） Hedgerow of Chinese juniper shrub, Meiji-mura, Aichi prefecture

カイズカイブキの列植 Hedgerow of Chinese pyramid juniper

○タマイブキ

高さ10mに達するイブキの挿し木苗を40cm内外の半球形に仕立ててこの名があり、植込地周りや土坡上に列植されている。強剪定をしなければ葉は丸味のある鱗片葉で優美である。積雪に弱いのが難点である。

● **Chinese juniper shrub**

Shown here are shrubs grown from cuttings of Chinese juniper trees (which themselves grow to heights of 10 meters) that were trained into hemispherical shapes about 40 centimeters tall. They are useful in gardens and atop stone fences. If not pruned heavily, they will develop beautiful rounded cataphylls. Unfortunately, these shrubs do not do well in heavy snow.

タマイブキの列植（長野県・松本市・旧開智学校）　Hedgerow of Chinese juniper shrub, former Kaichi School, Matsumoto, Nagano prefecture

タマイブキの列植（長野県）　Hedgerow of Chinese juniper shrub, Nagano prefecture

セイヨウツゲの列植　Hedgerow of Boxwood

イヌツゲの内垣（京都府立植物園）　Japanese holly interior hedge, Kyoto Botanical Garden

イヌツゲの列植（東京都・世田谷区・砧）　Hedgerow of Japanese holly, Kinuta Setagaya-ku, Tokyo

キャラボク玉の列植（愛知県・明治村）　Hedgerow of Japanese yew, Meiji-mura, Aichi prefecture

カンツバキの列植（京都府立植物園）　Hedgerow of winter camellia, Kyoto Botanical Garden

マメツゲとサツキの列植（千葉県・八千代市）　Hedgerow of Japanese littleleaf ilex and Satsuki azalea, Yachiyo, Chiba prefecture

イヌツゲの列植　Hedgerow of Japanese holly

すそ植え　Apron Hedges

セイヨウツゲのすそ植え（東京都庁）　Apron hedge of Ilex, Tokyo Metropolitan Goverment Office

サツキのすそ植え（埼玉県・所沢市役所）　Satsuki azalea apron hedge, Tokorozawa City Office, Saitama prefecture

○ **キャラボク**
外柵や建物の基部沿いに列植される低木は，その安定感と美装に役立つ効果を示してくれる。キャラボクはイチイに似た針葉樹で，葉は羽状に付かないで螺旋状で密生する点と高木化しない点が異り，刈り込み品が多い。

○ **ナリヒラダケ**
稈と呼ばれる茎の節部から小枝が間近かに群生していて大名竹の名でも呼ばれ，家屋の窓ふさぎとして列植することが多い。黄白色の縦縞が葉に入る斑入種も使われている。

● **Japanese yew (*Taxus cuspidata* var. *umbraculifera*)**
  Rows of short shrubs give a sense of well-appointed stability when used as outer borders or along house foundations. The Japanese yew (also called aloeswood), shown here, produces leaves in a dense spiral pattern and does not grow tall. It is very useful as a trimmed hedge.

● **Narihira bamboo**
  This slender variety of bamboo grows dense branchlets from its nodes, making it useful in blocking off windows from view. A popular variety has leaves with light yellow stripes.

キャラボクのすそ植え（東京都・世田谷区）　Japanese yew apron hedge, Setagaya-ku, Tokyo

ナリヒラダケの生垣　Narihira bamboo hedge

ナリヒラダケのすそ植え　Narihira bamboo apron hedge

ユキヤナギの列植（愛知県・緑化センター）　Spirea hedgerow, Green center, Aichi prefecture

ユキヤナギの列植（東京都・立川市・国営昭和記念公園）　Spirea hedgerow, Showa Kinen Park, Tachikawa, Tokyo

○ユキヤナギ

バラ科の落葉低木であり，枝は四方に放射状に垂れて春に小花を枝全体に咲かせ，雪が花に変わったような満開ぶりを見せる。葉は長さが2～3cmの柳に似た形をしている。刈り込まない自然形が美しい。

○**セイヨウアジサイ**

梅雨時の花として親しまれているアジサイの欧州で改良された種類で，花房も大きく萼片の色も多様である。日本種に比べてやや寒さに弱いが，東京辺りでも庭で育つ。花芽は10月中旬につくので開花後に間引き剪定をする。

○**アオキ**

常緑性の低木で陰地に向くために用途が広く，このような使用例もある。一見駄木と思われ勝ちであるが，葉の形の変化や斑入模様が多く，また雌の株であれば冬季間，赤い実が付いて観賞価値に多様さがある。

セイヨウアジサイの列植　Hydrangea (*Hydrangea spp.*) hedgerow

ユキヤナギとアオキの列植（東京都・小金井公園）　Hedgerow of Sirea and Aucuba, Koganei Park, Tokyo

● **Spirea (*Spiraea thunbergii*)**

A deciduous shrub and member of the rose family, the spirea produces branches that slant downwards in all directions from the trunk ; in the spring, flowers cover the entirety of the branches, making them appear as if they are covered with snow. The leaves are 2—3 centimeters long, shaped like willow leaves. Spireas look best untrimmed.

● **Hydrangea (*Hydrangea spp.*)**

The hydrangea is well known in Japan as a shrub that blooms during the rainy season. Shown here is an improved European variety, which typically has large corollas and sepals of various colors. Although not quite as resistant to cold as the Japanese variety, people in the Tokyo area cultivate it in their gardens. Buds appear in late October, so prune this plant shortly after it finishes blooming.

● **Aucuba (*Aucuba japonica*)**

Growing well in shady areas, this evergreen shrub has numerous uses. Although aucubas may appear to be commonplace shrubs, they have leaves with various shapes and color patterns, and female plants bear red fruit during the winter.

リュウゼツランとアツバキミガヨランの列植　Hedgerow of *Agave americana* and *Yucca recurvifolia*

二段垣　Two-Tiered Hedges

ベニカナメ（レッドロビン）（下段）の二段垣　Two-tiered hedge of red robin and Hirado azalea

○ ベニカナメ（レッドロビン）とヒラドツツジの二段垣

生垣には間を離して並列させる二重垣様式があり、この写真は上下差がある二段垣といえる。赤い葉を背景にして下部で花を観賞できるという植栽方法である。空石積みの目地植えも壁被用として効果的である。

○カイズカイブキ段づくり

イヌツゲに準じた枝づくりがなされ、直立的で高い仕立て方を示している。

● **Two-tiered hedge of red robin (*Photinia glabra f. red robin*) and Hirado azalea (*Rhododendron weyrichii* X)**

A "two-layered hedge" has two hedges grown parallel to one another ; a two-tiered hedge, as shown here, is a special case, in which one of the hedges is taller than the other. Here, the red leaves of this variety of the Chinese hawthorn are contrasted with the flowers on the shorter azalea plants. The use of the azalea in the mortarless masonry joints is particularly effective.

● **Chinese pyramid juniper (*Juniperus chinensis* var. *kaizuka*)**

The branches of this hedge are trimmed in the same way as a Japanese holly ordinarily is. The hedge has a tall, erect appearance.

イヌツゲとサツキの二段垣　Two-tiered hedge of Japanese holly and Satsuki azalea

カイズカイブキとイヌツゲの二段垣　Two-tiered Chinese pyramid juniper and Japanese holly

混ぜ垣　Mixed Hedges

○京都寂光院への登り段

大原の里には哀れみを誘う建礼門院が隠栖した尼寺があり、その門に至る石段傍には混ぜ垣が連なっている。名文の『平家物語』には、「ふるう造りなせる泉水木立、よしある様の所なり」とある。

●**Stairs up to Jakko-in nunnery, Kyoto**

The irregular stone stairway leading up to the *kenrei-mon-in* (Taira-no-Tokuko, daughter of Taira-no-Kiyomori) of the secluded Jakko-in nunnery in Kyoto is lined with a hedge of various plants.

カエデとサザンカの混ぜ垣（京都市・建礼門院）　Mixed hedge of maple trees and sasanqua at stairs up to Kenreimon-in nunnery, Kyoto

ピラカンサとドウダンツツジ，サツキ等の混ぜ垣　Mixed hedge of pyracantha, *enkianthus perulatus*, azalea

表1. 一般的な総角刈り生垣植物表

和名ほか	学名	科名	高	並	中	低
イチイ	Taxus cuspidata	イチイ	●	●		
キャラボク	T.c.var.umbraculifera	イチイ		●	●	●
カヤ	Torreya nucifera	イチイ	●	●		
ラカンマキ	Pedocarpus chinensis	マキ	●	●		
イヌマキ	P.macrophylla	マキ	●	●		
ナギ	P.nagi	マキ	●	●		
チョウセンマキ	Cephalotaxus drupacea var.koraiana	イヌガヤ			●	
ヒマラヤスギ	Cedrus deodara	マツ	●	●		
ドイツトウヒ	Picea excelsa	マツ		●		
クロマツ	Pinus thunbergii	マツ	●	●		
ツガ	Tsuga sieboldii	マツ	●	●		
スギ	Cryptomeria japonica	スギ	●	●		
ヒノキ	Chamaecyparis obtusa	ヒノキ	●	●		
サワラ	C.pisifera	ヒノキ	●	●		
ニッコウヒバ	C.p.var.plumosa f.	ヒノキ		●		
ヒムロスギ	C.p.var.squarrosa	ヒノキ		●	●	
カイズカイブキ	Juniperus chinensis var.kaizuka	ヒノキ	●	●		
ニオイヒバ	Thuja occidentalis	ヒノキ		●	●	
ヤマモモ	Myrica rubra	ヤマモモ	●			
マテバシイ	Lithocarpus edulis	ブナ	●	●		
アラカシ	Quercus glauca	ブナ		●	●	
シラカシ	Q.myrsinaefolia	ブナ		●	●	
ウバメガシ	Q.phillyraeoides	ブナ		●	●	
スダジイ	Shiia sieboldii	ブナ	●	●		
ヤブニッケイ	Cinnamomum japonicum	クスノキ	●	●		
ゲッケイジュ	Laurus nobilis	クスノキ	●	●		
イスノキ	Distylium racemosum	マンサク	●	●		
カナメモチ	Photinia glabra	バラ		●		
ベニカナメモチ	P.g.f	バラ		●		
レッド・ロビン	P.glabura f. Red Robin	バラ		●		
タチシャリンバイ	Rhaphiolepis umbellata	バラ		●	●	
タチバナモドキ	Pyracantha anguastifolia	バラ		●		
トキワサンザシ	P.coccinea	バラ		●		
ヒマラヤピラカンサ	P.crenulata	バラ		●		
カラタチ	Poncirus trifoliata	ミカン			○	
サンショウ	Xanthoxyum piperitum	ミカン			○	
ツゲ	Buxus microphylla var.suffruticosa	ツゲ			●	●
セイヨウツゲ類	B.sempervirens spp.	ツゲ			●	●
イヌツゲ	Ilex crenata	モチノキ		●	●	
モチノキ	I.integra	モチノキ	●	●		
クロガネモチ	I.rotunda	モチノキ	●	●		
マサキ	Enonymus japonica	ニシキギ		●	●	
フイリマサキ類	E.j.forma.	ニシキギ		●	●	
トウカエデ	Acer buergerianum	カエデ		○		
ブッソウゲ	Hibiscus rosa-sinensis	アオイ		○	○	
ムクゲ	H.syriacus	アオイ		○		
ツバキ	Camellia japonica	ツバキ	●	●		
サザンカ	C.sasanqua	ツバキ		●	●	
カンツバキ	C.hiemalis	ツバキ		●	●	
サカキ	Cleyera ochnacea	ツバキ	●	●		
ヒサカキ	Eurya japonica	ツバキ		●	●	
ハマヒサカキ	E.emarginata	ツバキ		●	●	
チャ	Thea sinensis	ツバキ		●	●	
ナワシログミ	Elaeagnus pungens	グミ			●	
ザクロ	Punica granatum	ザクロ		○		
ウコギ	Acanthopanax sieboldianum	ウコギ		○		
ドウダンツツジ	Enkianthus perulatus	ツツジ		○	○	
サツキ	Rhododendron indicum	ツツジ			●	●
キリシマツツジ	R.obtusum	ツツジ			●	●
ヒラドツツジ類	R.weyrichii spp.	ツツジ			●	●
セイヨウイボタ	Ligustrum vulgare	モクセイ		○	○	
オオバイボタ	L.ovalifolium	モクセイ		○	○	
ネズミモチ	L.japonicum	モクセイ		●	●	
トウネズミモチ	L.lucidum	モクセイ	●	●		
ギンモクセイ	Osmanthus asiaticus	モクセイ		●	●	
ヒイラギモクセイ	O.fortunei	モクセイ		●	●	
キンモクセイ	O.fragrans	モクセイ	●	●		
ヒイラギ	O.ilicifolius	モクセイ	●	●		
クチナシ	Gardenia jasminoides f.grandiflora	アカネ		●	●	
ヒトエノコクチナシ	G.j.var.radicans forma.simpliciflora	アカネ				●
ハクチョウゲ	Serissa japonica	アカネ				◑
ハナツクバネウツギ	Abelia grandiflora	スイカズラ			◑	
サンゴジュ	Viburnum awabuki	スイカズラ	●	●		
ホウライチク	Bambusa nana var. nobilis	イネ	●	●		
カンチク	Chimonobambusa marmorea	イネ	●	●		
ネザサ	P.variegata var. viridis f. glabra	イネ				●
オカメザサ	Shibataea kumasasa	イネ				●

注1） 学名は他の表とも『牧野日本植物図鑑』(1961)，『日本草本植物検索　III　シダ編』(杉本順一　1966)，『週刊朝日百科　世界の植物』(1978)，『最新園芸大辞典』(1983)，『朝日園芸百科　宿根草編　グランドカバー，芝，ササ類，コケ類』(1984)などによる。

注2） ●は常緑，◑は半常緑，○は落葉性を示す。

表2. 一般的な蔓生垣用植物表

和名ほか	学名	科名	巻き型	ひげ型	葉柄型	気根型	長枝型
イカダカズラ	Bougainvillea spectabilis	オシロイバナ					●
ビナンカズラ	Kadura japonica	モクレン	●				●
クレマチス類	Clematis spp.	キンポウゲ			○		
アケビ	Akebia quinata	アケビ	○				
ミツバアケビ	A.trifoliata	アケビ	○				
ムベ	Stauntonia hexaphylla	アケビ	●				
モッコウバラ	Rosa banksiae	バラ					◑
ナニワイバラ	R.laevigata	バラ					◑
ツルバラ類	R.spp.(Climing Rose)	バラ					○
ツルウメモドキ	Celastrus orbiculatus	ニシキギ	○				
ツタ(ナツヅタ)	Parlhenocissus trcuspidata	ブドウ				●	
トケイソウ	Passiflora coerulea	トケイソウ		○			
キヅタ	Hedera rhombea	ウコギ				●	
セイヨウキヅタ類	H.spp.	ウコギ				●	●
カロライナジャスミン	Gelsemium sempervirens	モクセイ	○				○
オウバイ	Jasminum nudiflorum	モクセイ					○
テイカカズラ	Trachelosperm asiaticum	キョウチクトウ	●			●	
クコ	Lycium chinense	ナス					○
ツリガネカズラ	Bignonia capreolata	ノウゼンカズラ		●			
ノウゼンカズラ	Campsis chinensis	ノウゼンカズラ				○	
アメリカノウゼンカズラ	C.radicans	ノウゼンカズラ				○	
スイカズラ	Lonicera japonica	スイカズラ	●				
ツキヌキニンドウ	L.sempervirens	スイカズラ	◑				
(洋種)スイカズラ	L.tatarica	スイカズラ	●				

草本類

和名ほか	学名	科名	巻き型	ひげ型	葉柄型	気根型	長枝型
ツルムラサキ	Basella rubra var. alba	ツルムラサキ	○				
フウセンカズラ	Cardiospermum halicacabum	ムクロジ		○			
スイートピー	Lathyrus odoratus	マメ		○			
ヨルガオ	Calonyction aculeatum	ヒルガオ	○				
アメリカアサガオ	Pharbitis hederacea	ヒルガオ	○				
アサガオ	P.nil	ヒルガオ	○				
マルバアサガオ	P.purpurea	ヒルガオ	○				
ルコウソウ	Quamoclit pennata	ヒルガオ	○				
ヤハズカズラ	Thunbergia alata	キツネノマゴ	○				

コケ（神奈川県・箱根美術館）　Moss at the Hakone Museum of Art, Kanagawa prefecture

カバープランツ
GROUND COVER

［Ⅰ］ 蔓植物について

　前記した蔓生垣と後に記す被覆用の各種植物と共に，多くの有用植物の中には蔓植物が多く含まれているので形態をまず示しておく。

1. 形態の種類

Ⅰ. 地上茎

(1)地這い型(匍匐茎)

　地表面を這い広がる接地生育を主とするが，中には次の上昇型を示す場合もある。広く造園，土木工事で地被用とするものが多い。

(2)上昇型(攀縁茎)

1)巻き型(纏絡茎)　他物に右，左，または左右不定に茎を巻き，上昇をする(例:フジほか)。

2)接着(気根)型　茎から吸盤，気根を出して，他物に付着し上昇する(例:ナツヅタ)。なお1),2)の両形態をなすものもある(例:テイカカズラ)。

3)ひげ型　枝や葉がひげ状を呈し，他物に巻き付き伸長する(例:ビグノニア，スイートピーほか)。

4)葉柄型　葉柄部で絡みつき上昇する(例:クレマチス)。

5)鈎刺型　茎に付着する鈎，刺状の突起物の助けを借り，他物に付着し伸長する(例:ツルバラほか)。

(3)走出枝型

　親株の下部から長い蔓状の走り枝を伸ばし，先端に新苗を生じる無性繁殖により繁茂をつづける(例:ユキノシタほか)。

(4)伸長枝型

　茎，枝が低く長く横に伸び，蔓状を呈する(例:オウバイ)。

2. 地下茎

　茎の一部は根茎となり地中を横走し，節部から地上茎を伸長させる(例:ヤブコウジ，ササ類ほか)。

2. 蔓植物の利用

　その生長力は旺盛で長く伸長し，また根も深く入り，繊維も長くて強靭な種類が多い。

　その利用は欧州では紀元前からブドウ酒用のヨーロッパブドウ系の栽培，そしてヘデラを愛の象徴としての祝婚用，また壁面植栽その他の利用が多い。「ジャックと豆の木」という英国の昔話も，天に高く伸びる蔓植物へのあこがれに発してのことかも知れない。アメリカのテネシー渓谷のダム化には，日本産のクズが被覆に役立ち，また地被類の研究と植栽も進んでいる。邦産野草のカナムグラが喜ばれているとの記事を読んだのは，昭和初期の科学雑誌であった。その利用法は何であったのであろうか。

　わが国でも蔓植物がいのち綱やシラクチヅルの吊り橋などに使われている。『日本書記』では庭師の路子工に芝春摩呂と呼んだという人があり，最も古い造園書の『作庭記』でも「しはをふせんには」と，芝の地被利用に触れている。以降，江戸期の大名庭園を経て，明治以後の芝生植栽が盛んになり，今日に至っている。

　「ふじ棚の水に映りし花の影　下より上に下りけるかな」とは一休禅師の作とされ，以前は松などに懸る藤の花の観賞がなされ，室町時代には藤棚造りが始められていた。アサガオ，ヨルガオの垣作り，ヒョウタン，ユウガオの棚作りは，納涼を兼ねて，庶民も古くから栽培をしてきた。

　野菜もマメ類，ウリ類，サツマイモ，ヤマイモなどがあり，繊維利用の縄，綱，布，家具，工芸品も多様である。また近年は観葉植物ブームで，室内に多くの蔓植物が飾られ，エキゾチックな観賞がなされている。

　造園や園芸の好きな人たちは熱帯地を訪れて，その生態と利用法を知り，奔放なその自然味に触れれば，その視野が広まり，楽しみも一層増すことであろう。そして，これらの中で地被，壁被，上被などの被覆利用が，現在では土木，造園上で多く利用されるに至っている。

［Ⅱ］ 被覆植物について

　被覆植物とは地上茎による蔓植物，ササ類等の地下茎などによる横走性植物と，コケ類と呼ばれる低く密生する蘚苔植物，ハイビャクシンのような低横臥性植物など，自体の性状により低く蔓延し，地被，壁被，上被(棚被)用にされる植物たちを示すものである。西洋芝と呼ばれる一群は株立ち性が多く，常に刈り込みが必要であるが，被覆植物にしている。

Ⅰ. 地被類

　一般に地被植物(グラウンド・カバー・プランツ)と呼ばれ，地表面上を低く生長して広がり，造園，土木上の修景緑化と土壌保全などに大きな効用を果たしている。

(1)効用

1)裸地広場の修景緑化。その低い生長による広がりは，柔軟な膨らみを呈して地表を美化する。

2)傾斜地，切り通しなどの斜面の風雨などによる侵食，崩落による土砂の流出の防止。

3)土埃り，飛砂，泥濘の防止。

4)照り返しなどによる微気象変化の緩和など温・湿度の調節。

5)雑草の防止。

6)景観展望上の視野の拡大化，道路側部斜面の見通しの良化。

7)道路のガードレール，中央分離帯，高架下の緑化。

8)樹下，庇陰地の被覆植栽。日照地に限る芝生地以外は陰地，半陰地を好む種類が多い。

9)運動施設の被覆植栽。踏圧に耐える芝類が用いられる。

10)災害時の非常避難地用。

11)屋上庭園の緑化用。

12)大規模な住宅地の造成利用。

(2)地被植栽の条件

1)宿根性であり，常緑性が好ましく，強健で繁茂力が旺盛であり，密生すること。

2)病虫による被害が少なく，有毒なガス，酸性雨などの公害に抵抗力があること。

3)匍匐または低横臥性であり，外観上高さが低いこと。なお上昇型の蔓植物ではなく，地這型，走出枝型など，他の樹木に登攀しない植物が適している。

4)被覆地には単一種を植栽して均整な外観美を呈することが望ましい。

5)種類の選択に当たっては，陽・陰地別，耐乾・耐湿性，耐熱性，耐潮性などを考慮し，適地に適種を用いる必要がある。

6)日本芝のような踏圧に耐えるものと，観賞本位のものとに大別される。

7)維持管理上で刈り込みなどの諸作業が絶えず伴うものと少ないものがある。

(3)植栽地の造成

1)適地の選択。広く展望のよい区域が好ましく，一般に視点上から眺望や俯瞰できる高さが適している。

2)畑跡のような良土で耕作されていた土地が最適であり，道路，工場，家屋跡地などは地中から瓦礫ほかの夾雑物，笹などの根などを除去する。また化学物質，過アルカリ，酸性，ヘドロ，粘質で植物に適さない不良土は掘り上げて良土を入れる必要があり，さらに通気，透水，保水力を適度にするために，有機質化への腐葉土や改良剤などの混入が望まれる。

3)整地に当たっては計画の高さにより，滞水しないよう僅かな自然勾配をつける必要がある。その深さは植物により異り，芝生でも15cmの耕耘をしたい。なおブルドーザーなどを使う場合は，計量の機械を使わないと固質化の恐れがある。

3)植栽は3〜4月が適期であり，日本芝は切り芝，他の草木類は鉢作りの苗をおよそ30cm間隔以上を基準として植え十分に灌水をする。

4）その後の管理は灌水と除草を継続し，生長に応じて必要な剪定と施肥を行う。

(4)管理

過度の伸長や密生を防ぐ剪定が必要である。イワヒバ科に属し蔓状に這うクラマゴケや蘚苔植物のコケ類は，直射日光が当たらない空中湿度が保てる場所向きで，水分管理とゼニゴケや雑草抜きをし，冬季は霜，雪などから守るために上部に松葉などを敷くと美しくも見える。なお美しいコケをふやすには，表土の1～2cmに焼いて消毒した赤土を敷き，張り付けるか上部に播くか，または胞子の散布による方法もある。

２．壁被類

石積み，コンクリート擁壁，石材質の建物の壁面，コンクリート質の棚，石塀の壁面などを被覆するもので，下部よりの接着型，上部からの地這い型下垂の蔓植物を用いる。

(1)効用
1）壁面緑化という用語があるように，無機的な鉱物質面を緑葉で飾り，美化をする。
2）暑熱，寒冷に対する微気象変化の緩和。
3）騒音の緩和。

(2)植栽
苗を壁面の下部または上部，ときに大きい擁壁では中間部に植え付け部を設けて植える。また垂直壁面に直接に張り付けないで，やや離してトレリス，フェンスなどを立てて，蔓植物を上昇させ，間接的に前面を美化あるいは陰蔽などを行う方法もある。この場合は止め金具や結束により誘引し，多くの蔓植物を上昇生育させることができる生垣的な応用である。

３．上被類（棚づくり）

蔓植物の利用法の一つであり，立体的に柱を立てて上部に棚を設け，葉で覆い，その下部で日光の強い直射光や暑気をやわらげ，緑の装飾と休息，花や実の観賞，そして果実生産に役立つという植栽法である。

古代エジプトでは，庭の園路上に蔓植物を上部に誘引し，日蔭をつくる構築物が既に設けられていたという。死都ポンペイの廃墟の中からも，テラスの噴水上にブドウ棚らしい蔓棚が残されていた。

気候的に太陽の強い光線をうける地域，特にイタリアのような文化的な先進地では，中世以前からペルゴラと呼ばれるものが設置され，のちには庭園文化の一つとして他の国々にも伝えられて，現に洋風の家屋，庭園，公園などではパーゴラの名で親しまれてきている。その設置位置は，家屋であれば南側の陽光部のベランダ部に接続させて張り出させ，園外では通路上，ときには園亭として独立した緑亭的なものが，普通は落葉性の樹木を用いて設置される。またトンネル式に側面も含めて繁茂させる形態，長さが１m以内程度のアーチ的なものもこの類に入れることができる（例：ミヤギノハギ，ツルバラ）。

わが国で庭の設備として設けられたのは恐らく藤棚からのことであろう。丸太で柱を立てて桁で骨組みをし，上部を竹で碁盤目状に結束した建て方は如何にも日本趣味的であり，石材柱，角木材を用いたパーゴラが如何にも装飾的，整型式であることに比べて，趣向的な違いが見られる。家屋の窓辺にブドウ，ヒョウタン，ヘチマなどを植えて絡ませ賞するのも，和趣味的な園芸棚といえる。

既述の『農業全書』では，産業上から瓜のトウガン，ヒョウタン，別にヤマノイモ，ブドウの項で棚の利用が記されていて，元禄時代にはすでに利用されていたことがわかる。さらに遅れて上梓された大蔵永常による『広益国産考』(弘化元年，1844)では，ブドウ棚，ナシ棚が図示されている。

ヨーロッパでのブドウの栽培目的は主としてブドウ酒用であり，成果品は外観よりは実収本位であって，普通は株立ち列植栽培であり，日本のような生食用の棚づくりは一般的ではない。中央アジアでも同様な栽培地を見たことがあるが，近年のシルクロードの紀行文には，天山々脈西方のフェルガーナ盆地で高い棚にブドウが実り，その樹陰で人々が休らう風景が記されている。夏が暑く乾燥の激しい地域では，その緑陰と実の生食が貴重なオアシスなのであろう。日本ではブドウ，フジなどが駐車場覆いに植栽されているのが近年の使用例に入る。家庭園芸ではキウイ，ツルレイシの植栽棚，ツルバラの高さ60cm位の低いベッドづくりも仕立て方の一型として見られるようになってきている。なお蔓植物ではない梨の棚づくりも周知されているが，東京都江戸川区内善養寺境内のクロマツは高さ1.8mほどで横に分枝誘引し，長さ約28mずつ棚状に広げて奇観を呈し，都の天然記念物に指定されている。

棚仕立ての長所としては，植え付け地は小面積でよく，上部に伸ばして生長蔓延させることにより，棚下に空地を得ることから，緑陰を下部で楽しめる休養の場が得られ，さらにその半陰地に合う鉢物類や庭用の被覆植物などや下草類の鉢栽培，挿し木苗床の設置などの兼用，鶏の放飼，自動車などの置場としても利用可能なこと，また面的な緑化と共に葉，花，実を強風から守り，生育の保護と傷みのない成果品の観賞，収穫をあげることができる。

栽培に当たっては，あらかじめ苗の植え付け地は長くなる根のために深耕をして良土に堆肥を混入し，元肥を入れると共に，生長段階に応じてチッ素，リン酸，カリ肥料の追肥をはかる必要がある。また棚上の枝の適当な配置と冗枝の剪定，さらに木本の場合は，枝の更新をはからねばならない。

江戸末期のナシ棚（『公益国産考』天保15年より）

江戸末期のブドウ棚（『公益国産考』天保15年より）

[I] Vines and Vinelike Plants

Vine plants (as well as plants that are not classified as vines but that spread in similar ways) can be used widely in gardens, as noted in the hedge and ground cover sections of this book. Many varieties grow rapidly, with long, sturdy vines and deep roots. The characteristics and uses of these plants are described in further detail in this chapter.

⟨A⟩ Types of Vine Plants

1. Plants with Above-Ground Stems

(1) Creepers

Creepers, as their name implies, spread along the earth. Some are also climbers (next category). They are widely used as ground cover in gardens and public-works projects.

(2) Climbers

Climbers are vine plants that grow upward on other objects. There are several subtypes:

- Twiners. These plants twine around objects as they climb; depending on the species, they may twine to the left, to the right, or in either direction. An example is the wisteria.
- Plants with suckers or aerial roots that attach to objects. Various kinds of ivy belong to this group. Some plants in this group are both creepers and climbers.
- Plants with beard-shaped branches or leaves that coil around objects as the plant lengthens. An example is the bignonia.
- Plants whose leaf stems twine around objects as the plant climbs. An example is the clematis.
- Plants with thorns or barbs that attach to objects as the plant lengthens. Ramblers (climbing roses) belong to this group.

(3) Vinelike plants with independent runners

These plants send out long, independent vinelike branches from the base of the parent root; buds at the tip produce luxuriant growth. An example is the creeping saxifrage.

(4) Vinelike plants with long stalks and branches

These plants grow long, low-lying vinelike branches and stems. An example is the winter jasmine.

2. Plants with Rhizomes

Some vine plants have rhizomes (a subterranean stem), from the nodes of which above-ground stems grow. Examples are the spearflower and bamboo grasses.

⟨B⟩ Uses of Vine Plants

Grape vines were grown in Europe before the Christian era, for the ultimate purpose of making wine. Ivy had numerous uses, including covering outer walls, where it symbolized love.

The kudzu vine is used in the southern United States——notably in the area around the Tennessee Valley Dam——the Japanese kudzu vine is used for ground cover and soil stabilization. Other vines native to Japan, including the Japanese hop (*Humulus japonicus*), have been studied in the West for possible ground cover applications.

Vines have appeared in different forms in literature. England has its tale of "Jack and the Beanstalk." In Japan there are old stories of vines used as lifelines and suspension bridges. The fifteenth-century Zen priest Ikkyu has attributed to him a tanka——

The flowers

on the wisteria trellis
reflected in the water:
Are they hanging upward
from below?

——from which we learn that it was at about this time that wisteria vines began to be grown on trellises; prior to this they had only grown naturally on pines and other trees.

Besides wisteria, from early times the common people grew various gourd vines, morning glories, and moonflowers on trellises and pergolas, to enjoy in the cool of the evening. Other vines——those of beans, melons, sweet potatoes, and yams——were used to make furniture and various craft items. People now grow vines indoors as house plants, giving an exotic touch to their rooms. A visit to the tropics will reveal further possibilities for vine plants.

[II] Ground Cover and Other Covering Plants

The term "covering plants" refers to ground cover, plants used to cover walls, and plants hung overhead on trellises and similar structures. This broad category includes vine plants, which spread by above-ground stems; bamboo grasses and other plants that spread by means of rhizomes; mosses; and low-lying shrubs such as the creeping juniper that spread over the ground. Lawn grasses, another type of ground cover, are used far more in the West than in Japan and are not described in detail here.

⟨A⟩ Ground Cover

1. Uses

Ground cover plants have numerous uses in gardening and public works projects, including soil stabilization as well as environmental beautification. The following are some specific uses:

- Covers otherwise bare open spaces
- Prevents erosion and collapse of soil on sloped land, such as that on the sides of a road cut through a mountain
- Prevents the formation of mud, dust, and blowing sand.
- Evens out small temperature and humidity changes that could otherwise result from reflected sunlight
- Prevents the spread of weeds
- Improves the visibility of scenic vistas and slopes on roadsides
- Adds greenery to guardrails and medians on roads
- Covers shaded ground (e.g., under trees, eaves) where grass generally grows poorly
- Covers the ground of recreational facilities. Varieties of grass able to withstand trampling are used.
- Used to cover the ground of disaster shelter areas
- Adds greenery to rooftop gardens
- Used in landscaping of large residential gardens

2. Selecting Appropriate Plants

Plants selected for ground cover should have the following characteristics:

- Perennial, preferably evergreen, plants that produce luxuriant growth
- Low-lying, creeping plants that will not climb up trees, walls, etc.
- Resistance to pest insects and, if appropriate, noxious gases (air pollution)

Additionally, plants should be chosen according to the

environment in which they will be placed: sunny or shady, dry or wet, hot, salty, trampled on (as in sports facilities) vs. simply looked at, etc. To create an even-looking view, a single variety of plant should be used in a given area. Finally, select plants according to the degree of maintenance you are able to provide: will a desired variety require frequent or minimal trimming, thinning, and other work?

3. Preparing the Ground

If possible, select a plot of land that will result in a pleasant view when looked at from the house or road. Land with good soil that has already been cultivated is ideal; otherwise, be sure to remove debris, old roots, and other stray matter from the soil. Soil that contains noxious chemicals or sludge, that is overly acidic or alkaline, or that is otherwise incompatible with healthy plant life should be dug out and replaced. To ensure proper air circulation and water drainage/retention, mix leaf mold and other organic matter into the soil. Create a gradual slope to ensure water drainage. (If it is necessary to use a bulldozer, use a light one to prevent the soil from hardening under the weight of the machinery.) Plant seedlings at least 15 centimeters deep (depth will vary with the plant).

Plant from March to April using potted seedlings (or plugs for grasses), spacing them at least 3 millimeters apart. Water plentifully. In the months following, continue to water sufficiently; weed, prune, and fertilize as necessary.

⟨B⟩ Wall-covering Plants

Climbing vines are used to cover vertical surfaces, including stone and concrete fences and house walls. Creeping vines may also be planted at the top of structures and allowed to hang down.

1. Uses

The prime use of wall-covering plants is to beautify what might otherwise be an unsightly inorganic surface. Such plants also help muffle sound and even out localized temperature variations.

2. Planting

⟨D⟩ Planting and Maintenance

There are several advantages to trellis planting. One is that only a minimal area of actual soil is required, leaving the ground free for other uses (a carport, garden pavilion, chicken yard, potted-plant nursery, shade-requiring ground cover, etc.) but at the same time allowing for the growth of a large, shade-providing plant. Fruit and flowers are better protected from wind than they would be on an ordinary tree.

Prepare the soil by stirring it up deeply, replacing poor soil with a good-quality variety if necessary. Mix in compost and perform an initial fertilization. You may eventually need to add nitrogen, phosphorus, and/or potassium fertilizer, according to the stage of growth of the plant. The vines will have to be directed into the positions you desire, and pruning will be required. For woody plants, trim stalks and branches yearly to ensure that they do not become overly thick and woody.

Plant seedlings at the bottom or top of a wall; with large retaining walls, seedlings can sometimes be planted in the joints of the wall. It is also possible to construct a trellis slightly separated from the wall and allow the plants to grow up on this, thus covering the wall indirectly. In this case, vines can be tied to the trellis to induce them to grow upward.

3. Maintenance

Prune wall-covering plants periodically to prevent overlong or overdense growth. Selaginellas, which crawl like vines, and mosses should be placed out of direct sunlight in an area of consistently high humidity; regulate water carefully and remove liverworts and weeds; cover with pine straw during the winter to prevent damage from frost and snow. For best results with moss, scorch the top 1-2 centimeters of red earth to disinfect it, and sow the moss spores over this.

⟨C⟩ Plants Hung Overhead

Vines may be hung on an overhead trellis supported by columns. Such an arrangement provides shade from the sunlight, lowering the temperature, and creates a relaxing space in which to enjoy the leaves, as well as any flowers or berries, on the vine. This is also, of course, how grapes are cultivated.

Overhead structures on which vine plants were grown, used for shade on garden pathways, are known to have existed in ancient Egypt. As noted previously, excavations of Pompeii revealed walls that contained depictions of plants on simple trellises (Figure 1). Pergolas——a kind of overhead trellis——were used in sunny regions, notably Italy, prior to the Middle Ages, from which they spread to other countries; they are commonly found attached to houses and in the gardens and parks of many countries. Pergolas attached to houses are usually found on the south (sunny) side, as extensions of a veranda roof. Similar structures are found over roadways and as garden pavilions (called arbors); these often use deciduous trees. Archways, about a meter long, covered with plants are another variation on this theme.

The Japanese version of the pergola is the wisteria trellis, traditionally constructed of upright round logs that support crisscrossing bamboo. This arrangement has a more distinctly Japanese flavor than pergolas constructed of stone pillars and squared timber seen elsewhere, which seem more decorative and formal. Other plants grown on trellises near house windows in Japan include grapes, gourds, and loofahs.

The 1697 work *Agricultural Compendium* mentions wax gourds, calabashes, yams, and grapes as being appropriate for growing on trellises. Okura Nagatsune's 1844 publication *Treatise on Domestic Production for the Public Good* depicts trellises of grapes and Asian pear-apples (the latter not a vine) (Figure 2, 3).

The ultimate purpose of growing grapes in Europe was wine making, not visual appreciation, and the grape plants have traditionally been grown upright, not on trellises. The situation is similar in parts of central Asia, although old Silk Road travelogues indicate that tall grape trellises were found in the Fergana Basin, west of the Tien Shan, and used as shady resting places. In Japan the use of grape and wisteria trellises as carports is a recent phenomenon, as are trellises of kiwifruit, balsam pears, and climbing roses. On the grounds of Zen'yo-ji temple in Edogawa-ku, Tokyo, there is a Japanese black pine (obviously not a vine plant) whose branches, at a height of about 1.8 meters, have been made to spread into an overhead trellis pattern, each segment about 28 centimeters long. This unusual arrangement has been designated by the Tokyo government as a natural monument.

地被類　Ground Cover

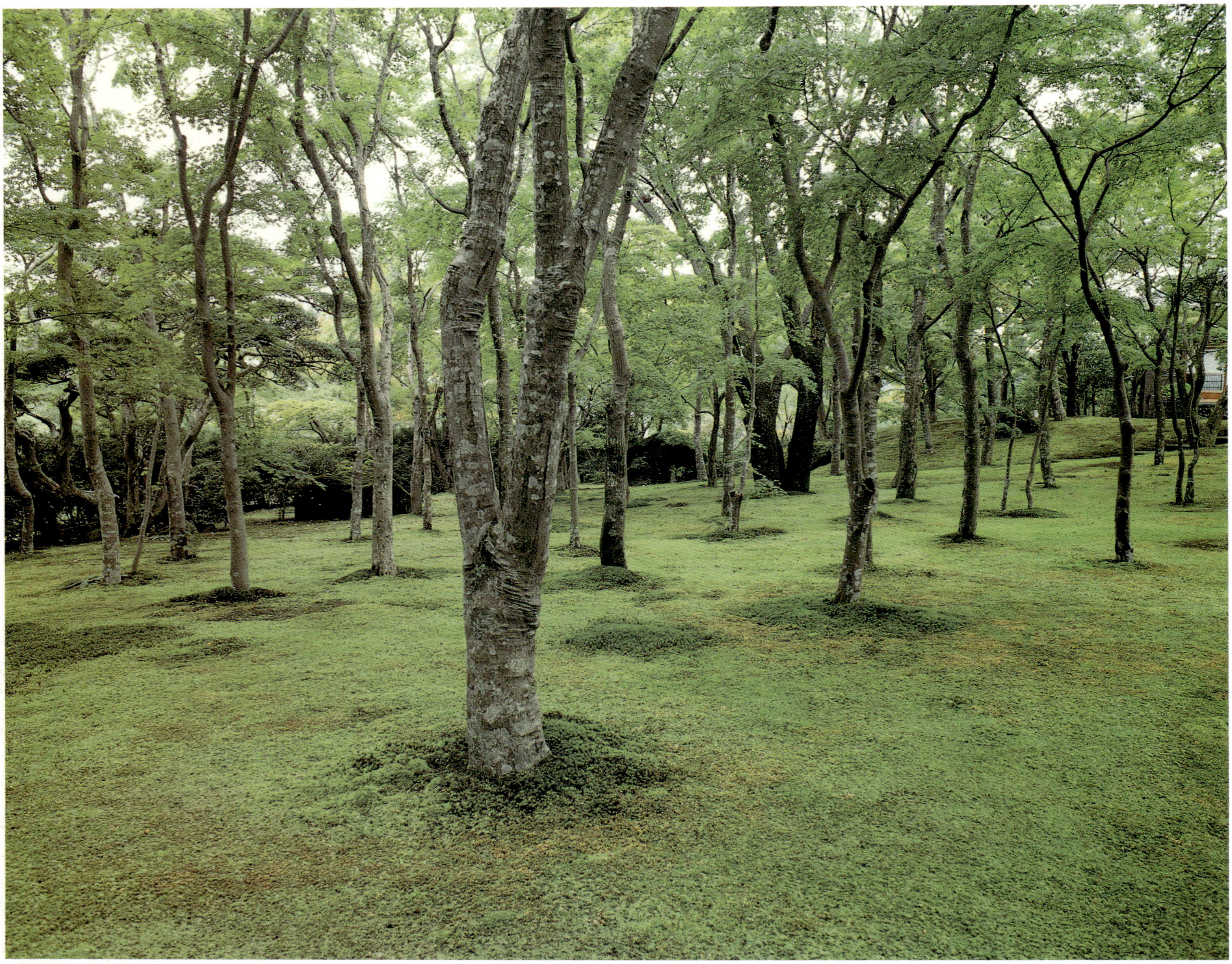

ヨツボコケほか（神奈川県・箱根美術館） Various mosses at the Hakone Museum of Art, Kanagawa prefecture

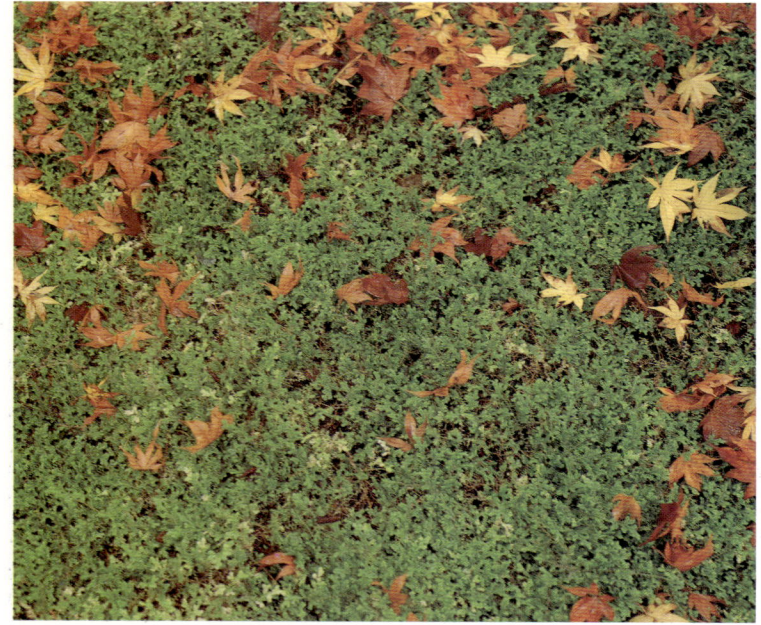

エイザンゴケ（クラマゴケ）（京都市・三千院） *Selaginella remotiflora*, Sanzen-in temple, Kyoto

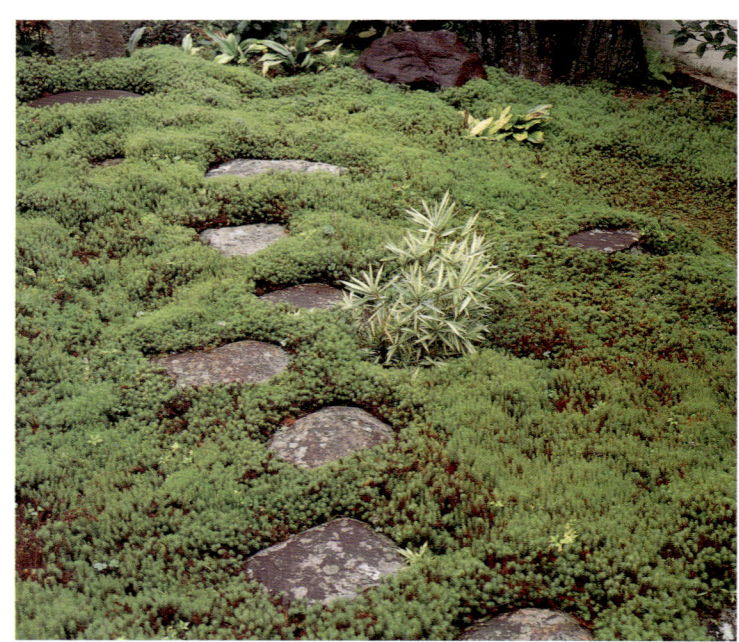

スギゴケ（京都市・寂光院） Hair moss at Jakko-in temple, Kyoto

○箱根美術館のコケ

神奈川県強羅にあり，この庭は山の斜面がややなだらかな場所に造られ，樹下にコツボチョウチンゴケ，エダツヤゴケ，ホソバオキナゴケ，オオスギゴケなどが見事に密生している。冬季はススキの葉で被覆している。

○エイザンゴケ（クラマゴケ）

イワヒバ科のシダ植物で主茎は1m余に伸び，多く分枝して地表面を這う。淡緑色を呈して柔軟であり，冬季は枯れ色を呈する常緑性で強健である。

● **Moss at the Hakone Museum of Art**

Various mosses, including Polytrichum formoum, grow densely under the trees on this gradual slope. Eulalia leaves are spread over the moss during the winter to protect it from frost.

● *Selaginella remotiflora*

The main stem of this hardy evergreen lycopod grows to a length of more than 1 meter and divides into many branches, giving the plant the appearance of hovering over the ground. The leaves are light green and pliable ; they turn yellowish-brown in the winter.

コケ（京都市・東福寺）　Moss at Tofuku-ji temple, Kyoto

スギゴケ（京都市・東福寺）　Hair moss at Tofuku-ji temple, Kyoto

スギゴケ（京都市・寂光院）　Hair moss at Jakko-in temple, Kyoto

スギゴケ（京都市・寂光院）　Hair moss at Jakko-in temple, Kyoto

ハイビャクシン　Creeping Japanese juniper

ハイビャクシン（東京都・立川市・国営昭和記念公園）　Creeping Japanese juniper, Showa Kinen Park, Tachikawa, Tokyo

ハイビャクシン　Creeping Japanese juniper

○ ハイビャクシン

対馬，壱岐，沖縄の海辺に自生する平臥性の針葉樹で，ソナレ（磯馴れ）の名もある。造園用には針葉性のものが多く使われ，石添え，池辺の植栽が多かったが，近年は道路中央分離帯，法面などへも利用されている。

● **Creeping Japanese juniper (*Juniperus chinensis* var. *procumbens*)**

This procumbent variety of the Chinese juniper, a coniferous plant, grows wild on Okinawa and nearby islands. It was traditionally planted around stones and on the banks of garden ponds; now it is also used on highway medians and shoulders.

ハイビャクシン（茨城県・水戸市・水戸植物園）　Creeping Japanese juniper, Mito Botanical Garden, Ibaraki prefecture

ハイビャクシン（名古屋緑化センター）　Creeping Japanese juniper, Green Center, Nagoya

ミヤマビャクシン　Sargent juniper

日本と朝鮮に産する常緑針葉樹で，主幹が横臥し枝が地表を這うよう低く伸長する。鱗状葉が表面に多く白緑色と呈し，下枝には針状の尖った葉が混じっている。陽樹であり，日当りのよい芝生地に適する。

● **Sargent juniper (*Juniperus chinensis* Line var. *sargentii* Henry)**

　This evergreen conifer grows in Japan and Korea. Its main stem lies flat, producing branches that cover the ground. Light green scalelike leaves are produced on the upper part of the plant, while the lower branches these and sharp needles. The plant is suited to sunny, grassy areas.

ミヤマビャクシンとオウゴンチャボヒバ　Sargent juniper and Darf cypress

ミヤマビャクシン（東京都神代植物公園）　Sargent juniper, Tokyo Metropolitan Jindai Botanical Park

ミヤマビャクシン（埼玉県・浦和市）Sargent juniper, Urawa, Saitama prefecture

ミヤマビャクシン（名古屋市緑化センター）Sargent juniper, Green Center, Nagoya

ツルニチニチソウ（東京都神代植物公園） Periwinkle(*Vinca minor*), Tokyo Metropolitan Jindai Botanical Park, Tokyo

シバザクラ（神奈川県・伊勢原） Moss pink, Isehara, Kanagawa prefecture

シバザクラ（北海道・紋別郡・滝上町） Moss pink, Takinoue-cho, Monbetu-gun, Hokkaido

○ツルニチニチソウ

中部ヨーロッパの原産の常緑性多年草で葉は革質の狭い長卵形で小さく、葡匐しながらよく発根し、強健でよく繁茂する。着花茎は短く直立し、春に紫色の径2cm位の高盆状の花を付ける。

○シバザクラ

北アメリカ東部原産の多年性草花で、葉長が1cm程の針状で茎は這い、分枝して広がり、春にピンク色の桜を思わせる花を一面に咲かせ、香りもあって美麗である。白，淡紫，濃赤の花もあり，近年は観光的な大植栽地が多い。

○アジュガ

ジュウニヒトエの名で呼ばれることが多いが、実はヨーロッパ原産の別種であり，蔓性で春に青紫色の花を付ける。半日陰の湿度のある土地を好み，常緑性であり，冬季には葉が赤紫色を呈する。

○アメリカツルマサキ

ツルマサキに似て小さい葉を付け，葡匐枝を伸ばして地上を這い，また気根により壁面などにも付着して上昇し広がる。アメリカでは何種かの変種を庭園の地被用にしている。

○フクリンツルニチニチソウ

南ヨーロッパ，北アフリカに原産する常緑の多年草で，葉は卵状披針形で対生する。無花茎は蔓になり，80cmほどに地を這い伸びて，葡匐または下垂用に適している。着花茎は立ち，春に淡青色の花を付ける。

● Periwinkle (*Vinca minor*)

This variety of the periwinkle, native to central Europe, has long, narrow ovate leaves with a leathery texture. It is a hardy plant, with numerous roots emerging from the creeping vine. In the spring, the short, erect flower stalks produce purple flowers 2 centimeters in diameter.

● Moss pink (*Phlox subulata*)

A perennial native to eastern North America, the moss pink forms sprawling mats. It has needlelike leaves and fragrant pink flowers that look like cherry blossoms; some varieties have white, lavender, or dark red flowers.

● Ajuga (*Ajuga*)

Also called bugles, these evergreen vine plants are native to Europe. They prefer partially shaded, moist ground. Their leaves turn reddish purple in the winter. In the spring the ajuga produces deep purple flowers.

● Euonymus (*Euonymus fortunei* "Emerald")

This creeping vine has small leaves, as well as aerial roots that allow it to grow on walls. Numerous varieties of the euonymus are planted as garden ground cover in the United States.

● Periwinkle (*Vinca major* var.)

A perennial evergreen native to southern Europe and North Africa, this variety of the periwinkle has long ovate flowers in an opposite arrangement. Its nonflowering vines grow along the ground to lengths of about 80 centimeters. Since the vines produce no roots, the plant is appropriate for hanging down from objects. Light blue flowers bloom from perpendicular flower stalks in the spring.

アジュガ（神奈川県・鎌倉市・東慶寺）　Ajuga, Tokei-ji temple, Kamakura, Kanagawa

アジュガ（札幌市・百合ヶ原植物園）　Ajuga, Yurigahara Botanical Garden, Sapporo

チョウジカズラ（東京都・千代田区）　*Trachelospermum asiaticum*, Chiyoda-ku, Tokyo

フイリアメリカツルマサキ（山梨県・甲府市）　Euonymus, Kofu, Yamanashi prefecture

フクリンツルニチニチソウ（埼玉県・川口市立グリーンセンター）　Periwinkle (*Vinca major* var.), Kawaguchi Green Center, Saitama prefecture

オカメザサ（東京都・文京区・小石川後楽園）　Okame bamboo grass, Koishikawa Korakuen, Bunkyou-ku, Tokyo

オカメザサ　Okame bamboo grass

オカメザサ（東京都・駒沢公園）　Okame bamboo grass, Komazawa Park, Tokyo

オカメザサ（埼玉県・所沢市役所）　Okame bamboo grass, Tokorozawa City Office, Saitama prefecture

○オカメザサ
江戸初期に造園された東京の小石川後楽園内の小廬山の南側の斜面植栽であり、背景美を見せ、土面の崩壊も防いでいる。1m以上に伸びるが強い刈り込みに耐え、密集群落し、その利用は多く、樹下の被覆植栽にも用いられる。

○アズマネザサ
箱根以東の陽地に多生する常緑または半常緑の多年草で、葉の長さ10cm以上、幅は1cm以上ある長披針形で先が鋭くとがる。高さは放置すると2m以上になるが、強い刈り込みに耐え、庭の広い地被の用もなしている。

○クマザサ
冬には葉の縁が白く枯れるために、隈笹の名があり、陽地・半陰地に群生し、耐暑・耐寒力も大きく、古来日本庭園の地被利用が多く、景観の主体もなしている。近年は葉がやや小さく矮性のコクマザサの利用もある。

● **Okame bamboo grass (*Shibatae Kumasaca* Makino)**
　The Okame bamboo grass here covers and reinforces the south side of a hill in Koishikawa Korakuen, a public garden in Tokyo laid out in the early Edo period. This variety of ivy prunes very well, growing densely to lengths of about 1 meter. It does well under trees.

● **Ground bamboo (*Pleioblastus chino*)**
　An evergreen or semi-evergreen perennial, ground bamboo grows prolifically in Hakone and points east. It has lanceolate leaves measuring about 5 by 1 centimeter. Although ground bamboo can grow up to 2 meters tall if left alone, it prunes down well and makes an attractive ground cover for a wide area of the garden.

● **Kuma bamboo grass (*Sasa veitichii* Rehd.)**
　This variety of bamboo grass grows well in both full sun and partial shade. Resistant to both heat and cold, it has long been used as a ground cover in traditional Japanese gardens. The edges of the leaves turn white in the winter. A dwarf variety with smaller leaves has become available in recent years.

クマザサ（東京都・国分寺市・殿ケ谷戸公園）　Kuma bamboo grass, Tonogayato park, Kokubunji, Tokyo

クマザサ（東京都・新宿区・京王プラザホテル）　Kuma bamboo grass, Keio Plaza Hotel, Shinjuku-ku, Tokyo

クマザサ　Kuma bamboo grass

クマザサ　Kuma bamboo grass

コクマザサ（山梨県・甲府市・文化センター）　Kokuma bamboo grass, Kofu Cultural Center, Ymanashi prefecture

コクマザサ（愛知県・緑化センター）　Kokuma bamboo grass, Green center, Aichi prefecture

コクマザサ（左）とチゴザサ（右）（山梨県・甲府市）　Kokuma bamboo grass, left, and *Pleioblastus fortunei*, right, Kofu, Yamanashi prefecture

コクマザサ（島根県・出雲）Kokuma bamboo grass, Izumo, Shimane prefecture

コクマザサ（東京都・井の頭公園）Kokuma bamboo grass, Inogashira park, Tokyo

アズマネザサ（東京都・文京区・小石川後楽園）Ground bamboo, Koishikawa Korakuen, Bunkyou-ku, Tokyo

オロシマチク（埼玉県・所沢市役所）*Pleioblastus distichus*, Tokorozawa City Office, Saitama prefecture

ヒメシマダケ（東京都・北区・赤塚植物園）　Ground bamboo, Akazuka Botanical Garden, Kita-ku, Tokyo

ヒメシマダケ（埼玉県・川口市立グリーンセンター）　Ground bamboo, Kawaguchi Green Center, Saitama prefecture

ヒメシマダケ　Ground bamboo

ヒメシマダケ（東京都・小金井市）　Ground bamboo, Koganei, Tokyo

○ヒメシマダケ

アズマネザサの品種とされ、フイリハコネダケともいわれる。葉に白い縞斑が入った長さ6～9cm、幅1cm位の披針形の葉を付け、生育旺盛で斑の入り方も多い。稈の高さは1～2mになるというが、庭内では刈り込んで30cm位にする。

●Ground bamboo (*Pleioblastus chino*)

This variety of ground bamboo has lanceolate leaves 6-9 centimeters long by 1 centimeter wide, with white stripes in various patterns. The stems can grow 1-2 meters tall, but should be kept to 30-50 centimeters tall in gardens.

フッキソウ（皇居）　Japanese pachysandra, Imperial Palace, Tokyo

フッキソウ（神奈川県立フラワーセンター大船植物園）　Japanese pachysandra, Kanagawa prefectural Ofuna Botanical Garden

フッキソウ（埼玉県・所沢市役所）　Japanese pachysandra, Tokorozawa City Office, Saitama prefecture

ディコンドラ（ダイコンドラ）（東京都・世田谷区・砧公園）　Dichondra, Kinuta Park, Setagaya-ku, Tokyo

○フッキソウ
山地の樹下に生える常緑の低木で，高さは20～30cm，葉はへら形で5～8 cmの長さがあり，輪状に互生し，春から夏の間に花穂を立てて白黄色の小花を密に開く。半日陰地に向き，やや湿度を好み，地下茎により繁茂
○ディコンドラ（ダイコンドラ）
北アメリカ南部に自生する多年性蔓草で，地上を2～5cm位の高さで生え広がる。葉は径が1～2cmの円形で長い葉柄で互生する。多湿な陽暖地向きで踏圧に弱く耐寒力も乏しいことから不踏地や目地植えに適する。

● Pachysandra (*Pachysandra terminalis*)
　Growing in mountainous regions, this shrub reaches heights of 20-30 centimeters. It spreads via rhizomes and has spatulate leaves 5-8 centimeters long in an alternate verticillate arrangement. Small white flowers bloom densely during the spring and summer. The pachysandra prefers partial shade and somewhat damp conditions.

● Dichondra (*Dichondra repens* var. *carolinensis*)
　The dichondra is a perennial vine that grows wild in southern North America, to heights of 2-5 centimeters. The oval leaves, 1-2 centimeters in diameter, have long stems arranged alternately. Dichondras are suited to sunny, warm, damp areas and do well in the joints of stone walls. They do not tolerate cold weather and being walked on.

ディコンドラ（東京都・中央区・銀座）　Dichondra, Chuo-ku, Tokyo

セキショウ（東京都・豊島区・目白公園）　Sweet flag, Mejiro park, Toshima-ku, Tokyo

セキショウ（東京都・墨田区・旧安田庭園）　Sweet flag, former Yasuda Garden, Sumida-ku, Tokyo

タマリュウ（チャボリュウノヒゲ）（埼玉県・川口市立グリーンセンター）　Dwarf Japanese snake's beard, Kawaguchi Green Center, Saitama prefecture

タマリュウ　Dwarf Japanese sanke's beard

○セキショウ

池や流れの縁に多い常緑の多年草で、葉は長さが30cm内外、幅は1.5cmほどの剣状でやや光沢があり、半垂れ状態で数葉が平らに並んで出る。水辺に用いることが多いが、乾きすぎなければ庭石、舗石の根締めにもする。

○リュウノヒゲ（ジャノヒゲ）

長さ10〜20cm位の細い常緑の葉を根生し、この名がある。陰地性で陽地にも耐え、匍匐茎による生長力が強く、地披・下草として定評がある。夏に淡紫色の小花を開き、後にコバルト色の7mm程の実を結ぶ。

○タマリュウ（チャボリュウノヒゲ）

ジャノヒゲの矮性種で、葉長は5cm位で短くよく密生して伸びがよく、濃緑の色彩美は目地植えなどとして利用度がふえてきている。また、葉刈り作業の手間をはぶくことができる。

● **Sweet flag (*Acorus gramineus*)**

The sweet flag is a perennial evergreen marsh plant with somewhat lustrous ensiform leaves 30 centimeters long by 1.5 centimeters wide. The leaves hang down partially, lining up to form a flat surface. Sweet flags can be planted near garden stones and pavement stones, as long as the area is not too dry.

● **Japanese snake's beard (*Ophiopogon japonicus*)**

The name "snake's beard" derives from the narrow, 10-20 centimeter long evergreen leaves that grow up from the roots of this plant. Used as both ground cover and undergrowth, it is a prolific plant, spreading by means of runners. Although suited mainly to the shade, it will also grow in the sun. Small lavender flowers bloom in the summer, which produce cobalt-colored berries.

● **Dwarf Japanese snake's beard (*Ophiopogon japonicus* f. *nanus*)**

This dwarf version of the Japanese snake's beard has deep green, densely growing leaves only 5 centimeters long. The plant is useful when grown in the joints of stone walls and around tree roots. It is a convenient plant in that the leaves need not be trimmed.

タマリュウとリュウノヒゲ（東京都・千代田区・帝国ホテル）　Dwarf Japanese snake's beard and Japanese snake's beard, Imperial Hotel, Chiyoda-ku, Tokyo

リュウノヒゲ（神奈川県・鎌倉市・東慶寺）　Japanese snake's beard, Tokei-ji temple, Kamakura, Kanagawa prefecture

タマリュウ（愛知県・緑化センター）　Dwarf Japanese snake's beard, Green center, Aichi prefecture

リュウノヒゲ（神奈川県・鎌倉市・東慶寺）　Japanese snake's beard, Tokei-ji temple, Kamakura, Kanagawa prefecture

リュウノヒゲ（東京都・立川市・国営昭和記念公園）　Japanese snake's beard, Showa Kinen Park, Tachikawa, Tokyo

タマリュウ（チャボリュウノヒゲ）（東京都・千代田区・御茶ノ水）　Dwarf Japanese snake's beard, Ochanomizu, Chiyoda-ku, Tokyo

タマリュウ（東京都・港区・新橋）Dwarf Japanese snake's beard, Shinbashi, Minato-ku, Tokyo

リュウノヒゲの目地植え（東京都・新宿区）　Joint platnting of Japanese snake's bear, Shinjuku-ku, Tokyo

セキショウ・アリスガワ　Sweet flag (*Acorus graminens* Soland.)

セキショウ・アリスガワ　Sweet flag (*Acorus graminens* Soland.)

ノシバ（東京都・立川市・国営昭和記念公園）　Zoysia, Showa Kinen park, Tachikawa, Tokyo

洋シバ（東京都神代植物公園）　Zoysia, Tokyo Metropolitan Jindai Botanical Park, Tokyo

○ノシバ

東京立川市にある昭和記念公園の立川口を入って直ぐに長くつづくモールに張られている風景であり，日本の山野に野生し，古くから芝地に張られてきた極めて強健な匍匐性の多年草で，粗剛感はあるが遠景的利用にはよい。

○コウライシバ

広く庭園，公園，運動場などの芝生に用いられ，強健に匍匐し美観を呈し，踏圧にも強い。陽地を好み，樹下や低湿地には不適であり，冬季には淡黄褐色を呈するが，園地を面的に明るく彩ってくれる。

● Zoysia (*Zoysia japonica*)

Shown here is the mall just inside the Tachikawa entrance of Showa Memorial Garden in Tachikawa, Tokyo. The sturdy variety of zoysia planted here grows wild in the Japanese countryside and has long been used for lawns. It has a somewhat rough look, but is useful in creating a sense of distant scenery.

● Mascarenegrass (*Zoysia matrella* Willd.)

Used widely in gardens, parks, and sports grounds, this variety of zoysia spreads well, doesn't succumb to trampling, and looks nice. Preferring sunny areas, it does not do well under shady trees or on low-lying, damp ground. It turns light yellowish brown in the winter, which may add a touch of brightness to a garden.

コウライシバ（東京都・文京区・六義園）　Mascarenegrass, Rikugien, Bunkyo-ku, Tokyo

シバ　Japanese lawn grass

コウライシバ（茨城県・水戸市植物園）　Mascarenegrass, Mito Botanical Garden, Ibaraki prefecture

ヤブコウジ（愛知県・緑化センター）　Spearflower, Green Center, Aichi prefecture

コクチナシ（埼玉県・川口市立グリーンセンター）　Dwarf cape jasmine, The Kawaguchi Green Center, Saitama prefecture

シロツメクサ　White clover

○ヤブコウジ

各地の丘陵地の林床に自生する常緑低木で，地下茎から高さ10〜20cm位に茎を伸ばし，長楕円形で先の尖った固い葉を数枚ずつ付ける。夏に葉腋から花柄を出し，白い小花を1〜2個咲かせ，秋から翌春まで赤い実を付ける。

○コクチナシ

中国原産といわれるクチナシの変種で，高さは30〜40cmで分枝が多く，葉は倒披針形で長さが4〜8cm，幅1〜2cmで両端がとがり，光沢がある。夏に径が3cm位の芳香のある白花を開く。本種は八重咲きで一重咲きもある。

○シロツメクサ

ホワイトクローバーの名で親しまれているヨーロッパ原産の多年草で，地を這い，3枚の小葉をつけ，葉柄は長く，夏には白い豆の花を多く球状に咲かせる。牧草にもなるが，腰をおろすと葉から青汁が出るので敷物が必要になる。

○シャガ

常緑性のアヤメの仲間であり，葉は幅が広くて光沢があり，根茎を伸ばして先端に子株を付けて地表を覆ってゆく。5月頃，花枝を出して径6cm内外の白紫色の花を数個ずつ開く。半陰地の被覆用として好適である。

● **Spearflower (*Ardisia japonica*)**

This evergreen shrub grows wild on the forest floor in hilly areas throughout Japan. Stalks 10-20 centimeters long grow out from the rhizomes, each producing several hard, oblong leaves with pointed tips. Peduncles grow out from the leaf axils during the summer, each blooming with one or two small white flowers. Red fruit is produced in the fall and lasts until the following spring.

● **Dwarf cape jasmine (*Gardenia jasminoides* var.)**

A variety of the native-Chinese gardenia, this plant grows to heights of 30-40 centimeters and branches out prolifically. The shiny oblanceolate leaves, pointed at both ends, are 4-8 centimeters long and 1-2 centimeters wide. Fragrant white flowers 3 centimeters in diameter bloom in the summer. This variety of gardenia has subvarieties with either single- or double-blossomed flowers.

● **White clover (*Trifolium repens*)**

Native to Europe, this pastureland perennial creeps along the ground, producing three leaves on each long stem and, in the summer, small white spherical flowers. If you sit on a bed of white clover, be sure to put a blanket down first, since a greenish liquid emerges from the leaves when they are broken.

● **Fringed iris (*Iris japonica*)**

The fringed iris is a relative of the blue flag, with shiny wide leaves and rhizomes that lengthen, sending out new stalks over the ground. Flower stalks emerge in May, each of which produces several light purple flowers about 6 centimeters in diameter. The plant does well as a covering of partially shaded areas.

シャガ（皇居）　Fringed iris, Imperial Palace, Tokyo

ツワブキ（東京都・墨田区・東京江戸博物館）Japanese silverleaf, Edo Museum of Tokyo, Sumida-ku, Tokyo

ハラン（東京都・墨田区・旧安田庭園）　*Aspidistra elatior* Blume, former Yasuda Garden, Sumida-ku, Tokyo

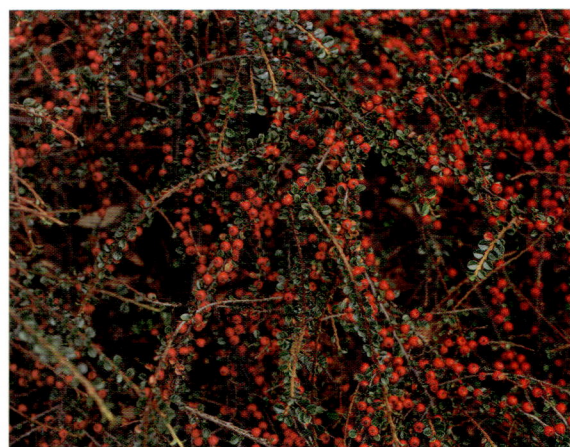

ベニシタンの実　Rock cotoneaster berries

ベニシタン（東京都・世田谷区・砧公園）　Rock cotoneaster, Kinuta Park, Setagaya-ku, Tokyo

コトネアスターの実　Cotoneaster berries

コトネアスター（横浜市・こども植物園）　Cotoneaster, Children's Botanical Garden, Yokohama

コトネアスター（東京都・新宿区）　Cotoneaster, Shinjuku Gyoen National Garden, Tokyo

○ **チョウジカズラ**

別名をセキダカズラとも呼ばれているテイカカズラの小葉品で，茎も線状で細い。各地の林下に多い蔓性木本で，気根により岩石・壁部に張り広がる。葉は長さが2.5cm，幅1cm前後の革質で赤変するものもある。

● *Trachelospermum asiaticum* var.

A woody vine usually growing under trees, this is a small-leafed (2.5 by 1 centimeter) variety of the plant described next, with fine stalks. It attaches to rocks and walls by means of aerial roots. The leaves have a leathery texture; some varieties turn red.

チョウジカズラ（セキダカズラ）（埼玉県・川口市立グリーンセンター） *Trachelospermum asiaticum*, Kawaguchi Green Center, Saitama prefecture

チョウジカズラ（東京都・新宿御苑） *Trachelospermum asiaticum*, Shinjuku Gyoen National Garden, Tokyo

フイリチョジカズラ（東京都・新宿区・京王プラザホテル） *Trachelospermum*, Keiou Plaza Hotel, Shinjuku-ku, Tokyo

マツバギク（川崎市・百合ヶ丘）　*Lumpranthus spectabilis*, Yurigaoaka, Kawasaki

南アフリカ原産で多肉質の茎，葉があり，よく分枝し，グラウンドカバー，石積み被覆などに用いられる。5～7月に径5cmほどの菊花状の紫紅色花を開く強健種である。

● *Lampranthus spectabilis*

A native of South Africa, this hardy plant branches out prolifically and so is useful in covering masonry walls and other surfaces, as well as the ground. It has fleshy leaves and from May to July bears deep crimson flowers 5-7 centimeters in diameter, in the shape of chrysanthemums.

ユキノシタの花　Saxifrage stolonifera Meerb

フイリヤブランとリュウノヒゲ（東京都・新宿御苑）　*Liriope graminifolia* and Japanese snake's beard, Shinjuku Gyoen National Garden, Tokyo

クサソテツ（東京都神代植物公園）　Ostrich fern, Tokyo Metropolitn Jindai Botanical Park, Tokyo

ナツヅタ（長野県・碌山美術館）　Boston jvy, Rokusan Museum, Nagano prefecture

○**ナツヅタ**

春から秋まで葉を出している冬季落葉性であり，見事な紅葉をして葉を
落とす。石面・他木に吸盤や気根を出して吸着し，洋館の壁面にも多く
用いられている。葉は光沢があり，密生し広く蔓延する。単にツタとも
いう。

● **Boston ivy (*Parlhenocissus tricuspidata*)**

The shiny green, densely growing leaves of this deciduous plant
turn a beautiful red in the fall. The vines of the plant attach
themselves to rocks, trees, and walls of houses by means of aerial
roots.

ナツヅタの紅葉　Boston ivy

カナリーキヅタ（東京都・世田谷区）　Algerian ivy

キヅタ　Japanese winter ivy

ナツヅタ（東京都・中央区・旧京橋小学校）　Boston ivy, former Kyobashi Primary School, Chuo-ku, Tokyo

○カナリーキヅタ

葉は長さ15〜25cm，幅10〜15cmある大形の葉で，3〜7浅裂する。茎には登上力もあるが，街路樹下や公園地の植栽地に植えて緑被面積の向上と美化に貢献している。品種数は多い。

○キヅタ

冬も葉があるためにフユヅタの名もある日本在来のヘデラである。幹枝からの気根の発生力が強く，他物への付着力も大きい。長じて幹枝が太くなるに従い，基部は壁体から離れてゆく。秋末に黄小花を開き，実は黒熟する。

● **Algerian ivy (*Hedera canariensis*)**

Algerian ivy has large leaves (15-25 centimeters by 10-15 centimeters) with three to seven lobes. Although it will climb vertical objects, Algerian ivy also serves well as a green ground cover. Many varieties are available.

● **Ivy (*Hedera rhombea*)**

The leaves of this variety of ivy last through the winter. Aerial roots grow out from its main vines and attach firmly to walls and other surfaces ; the main vines eventually grow thick, separating from the wall. Small yellow flowers bloom in late fall, eventually bearing black berries.

ヘデラ　Ivy (*Hedera spp.*)

セイヨウキズタ　English ivy

ヘデラ・ゴールドハート　Ivy

セイヨウキヅタ（左）とナツヅタ（右）（東京都・杉並区）　English ivy, left, Boston ivy, right, Suginami-ku, Tokyo

ナツヅタ　Boston ivy

ナツヅタ　Boston ivy

ヘデラ（東京都・銀座）　Ivy, Ginza, Chuo-ku, Tokyo

ナツヅタ（東京都・新宿区）　Boston ivy, Shinjuku-ku, Tokyo

ナツヅタ（東京都・豊島区・立教大学） Boston ivy, Rikkyo University, Toshima-ku, Tokyo

ヘデラ （神奈川県・カリタス女子短期大学） Ivy, Caritas Junior College, Kanagawa prefecture

ヘデラ （神奈川県・カリタス女子短期大学） Ivy, Caritas Junior College, Kanagawa prefecture

ヘデラ（東京都・港区） Ivy, Minato-ku, Tokyo

ナツヅタ（東京都・新宿区・早稲田大学） Boston ivy, Waseda University, Shinjuku-ku, Tokyo

ヘデラ（東京都・三鷹市）　Ivy, Mitaka, Tokyo

ヘデラ（東京都・三鷹市）　Ivy, Mitaka, Tokyo

ヘデラグレイシャー　Ivy

オオイタビ（東京都・世田谷区） *Creeping fig*, Setagaya-ku, Tokyo

ナツヅタ　Boston ivy

イタビカズラ　*Ficus foveolata* var. *nipponica*

○イタビカズラ
常緑性の蔓状低木で広く分枝し，気根を多く出して他物に密着し広く生育する。葉は革質で厚く，葉脈が隆起して目立つ。茎は浮かないでよく接着することから外観が美しく，ブロック塀の被覆に好適である。

● *Ficus foveolata* var. *nipponica*
　This evergreen viny shrub branches out prolifically, producing numerous aerial roots that attach firmly to surfaces. The vines stay close to the surfaces to which they are attached, giving this plant a particularly attractive appearance. The leathery leaves have protruding veins.

テイカカズラの柱被（東京都・港区）　Climbing bagbane Minato-ku, Tokyo

○ **テイカカズラの柱被**

パーゴラ（緑廊）の柱部の緑被であり，街頭の電柱にヘデラで被覆することもある。いずれも金網または鉄線で蔓の上昇を助けている。

● *Trachelospermum asiaticum*

　This vine plant is covering the columns of a pergola. A similar application would be utility poles. In either case, wires or wire mesh are needed to ensure that the plant will climb.

チョウジカズラ（京都市・大原）　*Trachelospermum asiaticum*, Ohara, Kyoto

フイリチョウジカズラ　*Trachelospermum asiaticum*

テイカカズラの花　Flowers of climbing bagbane

上被類　Trellis Plants

ミツバアケビ（東京都・墨田区・向島百花園）*Akebia trifoliata*, Mukojima Hyakkaen, Sumida-ku, Tokyo

アケビの実　Fruits of five-leaved akebi

ハトスヘデラ　Ivy

ヤマフジ（東京都・小金井市）Silky wisteria, Koganei, Tokyo

クズ（東京都・墨田区・向島百花園）　Kuzu vine, Mukojima Hyakkaen, Sumida-ku, Tokyo

キウイ（埼玉県・浦和市植物園）　Kiwifruit, Urawa Botanical Garden, Saitama prefecture

フジ（東京都・亀戸天神）　Japanese wisteria, Kameido-tenjin shrine, Tokyo

表3. 主なる被覆植物表

和名ほか	科名	地被用	壁被用 無目地	壁被用 有目地	上被用
タチクラマゴケ	Selaginella nipponica	イワヒバ	◐			
クラマゴケ	S.remotifolia	イワヒバ	◐			
コンテリクラマゴケ	S.uncinata	イワヒバ	◐			
ウラジロ	Gleichenia japonica	ウラジロ	●			
コシダ	Dicranopteris linearis	ウラジロ	●			
オオバノイノモトソウ	Pteris cretica	イノモトソウ			◐	
イノモトソウ	P.multifida	イノモトソウ			◐	
オニヤブソテツ	Cyrtomium falcatum	オシダ			●	
ヤブソテツ	C.fortunei	オシダ			●	
シシガシラ	Struthiopteris niponica	シシガラシ			●	
ヒトツバ	Pyrrosia lingua	ウラボシ			●	
タマシダ	Nephrolepis auriculata	シノブ	◐		◐	
ハイマツ	Pinus pumila	マツ	●			
ハイビャクシン	Juniperus chinensis var.procumbens	ヒノキ	●			
ミヤマビャクシン	J.c.var.sargentii	ヒノキ	●			
セイヨウビャクシン	J.communis	ヒノキ	●			
アメリカハイネズ	J.horizontalis	ヒノキ	●			
イタビカズラ	Ficus foveolata var.nipponica	クワ		●		
オオイタビ	F.pumila	クワ		●		
ヒメイタビ	F.thunbergii	クワ		●		
ヒメツルソバ	Polygonum capitatum	タデ	◐			
マツバギク	Lampranthus spectabilis	ツルナ	◐			
サネカズラ	Kadsura japonica	モクレン	●	●		
サギーナ	Sagina subulata	ナデシコ	○			
ニリンソウ	Anemone flaccida	キンポウゲ	○			
アケビ	Akebia quinata	アケビ				○
ムベ	A.hexaphylla	アケビ				●
ミツバアケビ	A.trifoliata	アケビ				○
ツルマンネングサ	Sedum sarmentosum	ベンケイソウ	○			
ユキノシタ	Saxifraga stolonifera	ユキノシタ	●		●	
アカエナ	Acaena buchananii	バラ	○			
アカエナ	A.microphylla	バラ	○			
ハゴロモソウ	Alchemilla alpestris	バラ	○			
—	A.alpina	バラ	○			
ポテンテイラ	Potentilla verna	バラ	○			
レンゲソウ	Astragalus sinicus	マメ	○			
シロツメグサ	Trifolium repens	マメ	○			
ミヤギノハギ	Lespedeza thunbergii	マメ				○
クズ	Pueraria thunbergiana	マメ				○
ヤマフジ	Wistaria brachybotrys	マメ				○
ノダフジ	W.floribunda	マメ				○
ノウゼンハレン	Tropaeolum majus	ノウゼンハレン	○			
フッキソウ	Pachysandra terminalis	ツゲ	●			
ツルマサキ	Euonymus radicans	ニシキギ	●			
アメリカツルマサキ	E.r."Emerald"	ニシキギ	●			
コバノツルマサキ	E.f.var.microphyllus	ニシキギ	●			
ナツヅタ	Parthenocissus tricuspidata	ブドウ		○		○
ブドウ	Vitis vinifera	ブドウ		○		○
キウイ	Actinidia chinensis	サルナシ				○
ヒッペリクム	Hypericum calycinum	オトギリソウ	○			
—	H.cerastoides	オトギリソウ	○			
カナリーキヅタ系	Hedera canariensis	ウコギ	●	●		
セイヨウキヅタ系	H.helix	ウコギ	●			
キヅタ	H.rhombea	ウコギ		●		
ヤブコウジ	Ardisia japonica	ヤブコウジ	●			
ヨウシュコナスビ	Lysimachia nummularia	サクラソウ	○			
オウバイ	Jasminum nudiflorum	モクセイ			○	
テイカカズラ	Trachelospermum asiaticum	キョウチクトウ	●			
セキダカズラ	（小葉種）	キョウチクトウ	●	●		
ツルニチニチソウ	Vinca major	キョウチクトウ	●			
ヒメツルニチニチソウ	V.minor	キョウチクトウ	●			
ソライロアサガオ	Ipomoea tricolor var.splendiscoerulea (Heavenly Blue)	キョウチクトウ				○
ダイコンドラ	Dichondra repens var.carolinensis	キョウチクトウ	●			
シバザクラ	Phlox subulata	ハナシノブ	◐			
リッピア	Phyla（Lippia）nodiflora var.canescens	クマツヅラ	○			
ヒメビジョザクラ	Verbena tenera	クマツヅラ	○			
ツルジュウニヒトエ	Ajuga reptans	シソ	●			
フイリカキドオシ	Glechoma hederacca subsp.grandis f.	シソ	●			
ラーミウム	Lamium galeobdolon	シソ	●			
イブキジャコウソウ	Thymus quinquecostatus	シソ	●			
ギンパイカ	Nierembergia rivularis	ナス	●			
シロバナサギゴケ	Mazus miquelii var.albiflorus	ゴマノハグサ	◐			
コクチナシ	Gardenia jasminoides var.radicans	アカネ	●			
ロニツエラ	Lonicera mitida	スイカズラ	●			
ヒョウタン	Lagenaria leucantha var.gourda	ウリ				○
ヘチマ	Luffa cylindrica	ウリ				○
ツルレイシ	Momordica charantia	ウリ				○
ハヤトウリ	Sechium edule	ウリ				○
ヒメノコギリソウ	Achillea tomentosa	キク	●			
アルクトテーカ	Arctotheca calendula	キク	●			
ツワブキ	Ligularia tussilaginea	キク	●			
フキ	Petasites japonicus	キク	●			
ウエデリア	Wedelia prostrata	キク	●			
エゾミヤコ	Sasa apoiensis	イネ	●			
アリマコスズ	S.arimagunensis	イネ	●			
ゴテンバザサ	S.asahinae	イネ	●			
フタタビコスズ	S.futatabiensis	イネ	●			
ウンゼンザサ	S.gracillima	イネ	●			
ヨナイザサ	S.kagamiana	イネ	●			
ヤネフキザサ	S.kurokawana	イネ	●			
センナンブスズ	S.myojinensis	イネ	●			
ミヤコザサ	S.nipponica	イネ	●			
チマキザサ	S.paniculata	イネ	●			
クマザサ	S.a!bo-marginata	イネ	●			
シロシマシイヤ	Sasaella glabra f.albostriana	イネ	●			
ハコネスズ	S.hisauchii	イネ	●			
コチク	S.hortensis	イネ	●			
コクマザサ	S.kogasensis var.gracillima	イネ	●			
オカメザサ	Shibataea kumasaca	イネ	●			
フイリクサヨシ	Phalaris arundinacea var.picta	イネ	●			
アケボノザサ	Pleioblastus argenteostriatus f.akebono	イネ	●			
アズマネザサ	P.chino	イネ	●			
ヒメシマダケ	P.c.'Flavo-variegatus'	イネ	●			
オロシマチク	P.distichus	イネ	●			
チゴザサ	P.fortunei	イネ	●			
ネザサ	P.variegatus var.viridis f.glabra	イネ	●			
カムロザサ	P.viridistriatus	イネ	●			
オオバヤダケ	Pseudosasa tessellata	イネ	●			
ノシバ	Zoysia japonica	イネ	◐			
コウライシバ	Z.matrella var.tenuifolia	イネ	◐			
ビロウドシバ	Z.tenuifolia	イネ	◐			
カンスゲ	Carex morrowii	カヤツリグサ	●			
セキショウ	Acorus gramineus	サトイモ	●			
ポトス	Epipremnum aureum	サトイモ	●			
シロフハタカラクサ	Tradescantia fluminensis	ツユクサ	●			
テンモンドウ	Asparagus cochinchinensis	ユリ	●			
ハナニラ	Brodiaea uniflora	ユリ	●			
オリズルラン	Chlorophytum comosum	ユリ	●			
スズラン	Convallaria majus var.keiskei	ユリ	●			
ドイツスズラン	C.majalis	ユリ	●			
リュウキュウヤブラン	Liriope gracilis	ユリ	●			
ヒメヤブラン	L.minor	ユリ	●			
ヤブラン	L.graminifolia	ユリ	●			
ジャノヒゲ	Ophiopogon japonicus	ユリ	●			
チャボリュウノヒゲ	O.j.f.nanus	ユリ	●			
オオバジャノヒゲ	O.planiscapus	ユリ	●			
キチジョウソウ	Reineckea carnea	ユリ	●			
シャガ	Iris japonica	アヤメ	●			
エビネ	Calanthe discolor	ラン	●			

注）●は常緑，◐は半常緑，○は落葉性を示す。

トクサ Scouring rush

下草
UNDERGROWTH

日本の庭園は以前から，その下層部の，主として多年草，ときに矮小な低木を下草と呼び，庭石ほかの石造の工作物，樹木の根締め，池や流れの岸辺，滝口，延べ段，飛び石の縁や目地，石積み，生垣下などの適宜な空地に，低小な数株を添え植えし，自然調で風致さを補助する景観を表現してきた。

その多くは野趣に富んだ常緑種を，高さ，幅，そして立体や面積的に主体である石や木の脇役的に添え，地表部から上の主役との接続と連結の役をなし，また生命の緑による修飾の用も加えてきている。

前述した地被類が広い面的植栽であるのに対して，下草類は1〜数株または小規模な点的な植栽であり，また陰陽の適地を選び使用植物も余り多くはなく，その位置も適宜に選択できる。

「春のもてあそびをわざとは植ゑで，秋の前栽をばむらむら(注:叢々，斑々)ほのかにまぜたり」と『源氏物語』が述べる六条院の光源氏の寝殿造りの邸の庭のように，平安の人々の心情が春に咲く華美な花々より，秋の静寂さを愛したように，下草の配植も巧むことなく自然調なたたずまいを感じさせるようにある姿が本来的なのである。

しかし近年は庭も洋風化が増え，日本庭園とは違う材料が使用されてきている。特に門から玄関に至る間の前庭部の装飾的な植栽のウエートが大きい。そして上部を広く明るく見せるために低木と下草の植栽が一般化されてきている。その種類が外来の洋種であったとしても，適切な選択による伝統的なセンスのある配植であれば，感性的に楽しみ深いものになる。

日本の従来の下草類としては，常緑性のシダほか一部の種類が親しまれて，地味で落ちつきのある庭趣の引き立て役をしてきた。近年は，花の美しいもの，斑入葉ものも使用され，またハボタンのような短期的な植栽も下草として扱われ，庭に明るい効果を出している。しかし，庭草と呼ぶ華美な草本類の過用では，それは花園であり，下草本来の使用効果とは異ることになる。

1．下草の選定と入手

(1)選定

まず，近辺の庭園で下草の種類と利用法とに関心を寄せることである。その植栽場所は前記の諸所で見られるであろうし，家の前庭，主庭，建物に囲まれた坪庭などの景観的な配植美も参考になり，また門柱の下の小さな植込み地の少数の下草も，道路からの外景として見応えがあるものである。

下草は一般に野生種が多く用いられてきていて，それぞれが適当な生育環境をもっている。例えば，多く用いられてきているシダ類の場合は，好日性(例:オニヤブソテツ，ヤブソテツ，ベニシダ)，陰地性(例:イノデ)，乾地性(例:タマシダ)などと分かれ，岩石上(例:イワヒバ)，樹幹上(例:ノキシノブ)，石積み目地(例：ヤブソテツ)などと生育地の違いがあることも知るべきである。

(2)入手法

下草類の生産は地被類と共用できる種類を除いては少く，入手は容易ではない。直接の山野での採集も困難であるから，所有者からの分譲か下草を知る業者に依頼をするとよい。

2．植栽と管理

適地に適作をまず考え，必要により保湿，通気をよくするために，腐葉土などを入れて地ごしらえをして，鉢作りの健全な苗を植え，しばらくは灌水をつづける。

管理にあまり手をかける必要はない。繁茂過剰で見苦しく繁雑になれば，助演品らしく大きさ，量を減らして主役を生かすように鋏を入れて抑制をするか株分けをする。蔓植物を使う場合も同様である。夏緑性で秋末に葉が枯れたら切り取るが，クサソテツ，イヌガンソクなどは，冬季間は胞子をつけた実葉が立つので観賞用になるから残すことにする。なお，夏の間の打ち水は，埃取りを兼ねて納涼感を高めてくれるものである。

Undergrowth

Japanese gardeners have long used undergrowth——usually evergreen plants such as perennial herbs (mainly) and dwarf shrubs (occasionally)——in various capacities complementary to taller or otherwise more significant garden elements: around garden stones and along stone walls, around trees to tamp down roots, along the banks of garden streams and ponds and at the top of waterfalls, along and in the joints of flagstone paths, and under hedges. Properly used, undergrowth enhances both the elegance and natural appearance of a garden and, when accompanying taller items, provides a connection between that item and the earth below.

Although "ground cover" and "undergrowth" both refer to low-lying garden plants, ground cover plants are those that spread and cover a wide area, whereas undergrowth plants are small varieties grown singly or in clumps. Various types of undergrowth are respectively appropriate to different sunlight and moisture conditions; moreover, each has an season appropriate for planting.

A line from *The Tale of Genji* ——"avoiding planting showy spring flowers in the garden [of Prince Genji's palace] in favor of autumn plants growing here and there"——attests to the Heian preference for the tranquility of autumn as against the showy flowers of spring, and also indicates that undergrowth plants were originally grown to provide a natural, uncontrived appearance. More recently, however, Western, nontraditional garden elements appear with greater frequency. In particular, front gardens, between the gate and the entrance to the house, often have extensive decorative plantings. Greater emphasis tends to be placed on showing off the taller garden elements, while using more "generic" shrubs and undergrowth. Even so, it is possible to select imported plant varieties to create a traditional arrangement that provides depth of enjoyment.

Undergrowth traditionally used in Japanese gardens includes various evergreen ferns and other plants, often wild ones, that evoke a sense of calm and restraint, thus setting off other garden elements. Recent additions to the undergrowth repertoire produce brighter results: flowering plants, plants with variegated leaves, and plants like ornamental kale planted for relatively brief periods of time. Overuse of such plants, however, results in a flower garden and tends to detract from the traditional results produced by undergrowth.

⟨A⟩ Selecting Undergrowth Plants

Acquiring undergrowth plants may be difficult, since few varieties are cultivated for sale, other than those used also as ground cover. You may be able to go out into the country to collect cuttings, but this is illegal in many areas. Perhaps the best means of obtaining undergrowth are to seek the advice of local experts and to have neighbors or acquaintances provide you with starter plants from their gardens.

The first step in selecting what varieties of undergrowth to plant in your garden is to look around at the gardens in your area to determine what local varieties exist and see how they are planted——in front gardens or main gardens, around buildings, around gate posts, and so forth. How do the plants look in their respective locations, and how do they look from the road?

As noted above, plants used for undergrowth tend to be wild ones, and each is appropriate to a specific environment. For example, some ferns prefer a sunny environment, whereas others prefer the shade; some like dry ground; some, like selaginella, grow atop rocks, while others, like the polypody, attach to tree trunks.

⟨B⟩ Planting and Care

After you have selected a plant appropriate to the site to be cultivated, let the seedlings establish themselves well in pots. Add leaf mold or other appropriate materials to the soil, as necessary, to ensure proper moisture retention and drainage; plant the seedlings; and water until well established.

Little care will be required once the plants are established. If the undergrowth plants (including vine plants) proliferate to the extent that they become unsightly, thin them out with clippers to a density befitting their supporting role. Clip off leaves from plants that will loose them in the autumn; leave on sporophylls (spore-bearing leaves) that appear in the winter, as these will be pleasant to look at. Sprinkling water around the area of ferns will heighten the sense of coolness during the summer.

下草 Undergrowth

コガネシダ（オウゴンシダ） *Woodsia macrochlaena*

メヤブソテツ *Cyrtomium fortunei*

○ メヤブソテツ

上野公園にある日本芸術院の背景に並ぶ桂垣には清雅さがあり，その下部の適所に場を選んで見える大きなシダはメヤブソテツであろう。葉長が80cmにも及ぶ常緑性でやや光沢があり，大きな下草として十分な存在価値を示している。

○ コガネシダ

盆栽愛好家が平鉢に低く寄せ植えをして楽しむ夏緑性のシダで，葉が黄色を帯びるのでオウゴンシダとも呼ぶ。東北地方以南の山地の岩上に産し，高さは10～20cm内外に根茎から叢生する。

● *Cyrtomium fortunei*

These large evergreen ferns have been placed here and there along the Katsura bamboo-branch fence that forms the backdrop to the Japan Art Academy at Ueno Park, Tokyo. The somewhat shiny fronds grow up to 80 centimeters long.

● *Woodsia. macrochlaena*

This yellow-leafed fern is a favorite for bonsai. It grows densely from rhizomes in rocky, mountainous regions on most of Honshu island, to 10-20 centimeters in height.

オモト（京都市・実光院） *Rohdea japonica*, Jikko-in temple, Kyoto

オモト（京都市・光命院） *Rohdea japonica*, Komyo-in temple, Kyoto

○**オモト**

林下に自生する常緑多年草で，短く横走する地下茎の先端から10枚前後の広披針形の葉を数枚開き，万年青の名のような安定感を示す。初夏に黄白色の花を短い花茎に咲かせ，冬季は赤い実を付けて冬庭の彩りを示す。

○**フウチソウ**

風にそよぐさまから風致草の名があり，長さ30～40cmで細い柄をつけた葉が叢生し，全形に趣き深さがある。石添えに植えると夏でも涼味を感じさせてくれる。裏葉草の名もあり，葉の裏面が表に出ていることからいう。

○**イノデ**

「猪の手」の名のように春に新葉が開く前には褐色の鱗片が付いていて野趣味がある。1葉の長さは0.8m近くまで伸び，濃い緑色で光沢があり，冬季も緑葉を残す強健種である。この仲間には種類と雑種が多い。

● *Rohdea japonica*

Growing wild under trees, this evergreen perennial sends out short, horizontally growing rhizomes at the ends of each of which are produced about ten short, sharp leaves. Pale yellow flowers are produced on short stalks in early summer, while red fruit in the winter adds color to the garden.

● *Hakonechloa macra*

Leaves grow densely on slender stalks 30-40 centimeters long, giving this plant an elegant appearance. When grown around stones, the plant provides a sense of coolness in the summer.

● *Polystichum polyblepharum*

In the spring, before new leaves emerge, this hardy plant has brown ramenta (scales), giving it a rustic appearance. The dark green, shiny leaves eventually reach 1 meter in length and live through the winter. There exist numerous varieties of this plant, as well as hybrids between it and others.

フウチソウ *Hakonechloa macra*

イノデ（皇居） *Polystichum polyblepharum*, Imperial Palace, Tokyo

コシダ（島根県） *Dicranopteris dichotoma*, Shimane prefecture

フイリヤブラン（東京都・国分寺市・殿ケ谷戸公園） *Liriope graminifolia* var.,
Tonogayato Park, Kokubunji, Tokyo

ハラン（京都市・実光院） *Aspidistra elatior*, Jikko-in temple, Kyoto

○コシダ

正月に飾るウラジロに似て葉は小さくて硬く，6枚の羽片がある。高さは0.6〜1m余り伸び，根茎も非常に長く伸びるので樹下の地被用として好適である。葉裏が白いために美観を呈する。

○フイリヤブラン

ヤブランの斑葉種で，両側に黄条が入りノシメランとも呼ばれる。秋には30cm程の花茎を立て，青紫色の小花を穂状につけて美しいので，一般に花壇などの縁植えにされている明るい感じの多年草である。

○ヤブラン

葉長40cm位で幅は1cm余の濃緑色の葉を広げる常緑多年草で半日陰地に繁茂し，9月頃に花茎を30cm余り立ててユリ科の青紫色の小花を穂状に多数開き，後に黒い実を付ける樹下林間向きの下草である。地被植栽もされる。

○ハラン

葉長が60cm余，幅が10cmもある大柄な常緑多年草であり，下草としては高い姿を示すが，その簇生するさまは茶庭をはじめとして日本庭園の下方部をよく引きしめてくれる存在である。花は春に地面際に咲き，目立たない。

● *Dicranopteris dichotoma*

This fern grows to heights of 0.6-1 centimeter, with small, hard fronds having six pinnae. The rhizomes grow very deep, making the plant appropriate for use as undergrowth below trees. The white undersurfaces of the leaves make this a nice choice for gardens.

● *Liriope graminifolia* var.

This evergreen perennial is a variety of the plant described next, with yellow stripes on both surfaces of its leaves. In the fall it sends out flower stalks about 30 centimeters long, on which grow small violet spikes. The plants provide a flower bed with a bright border.

● *Liriope graminifolia*

Flourishing in areas shaded during part of the day, this evergreen perennial, a member of the lily family, produces deep green leaves about 40 centimeters long and 1 centimeter wide. Numerous small violet spikes bloom from flower stalks 30 centimeters long that grow out in September ; black fruit forms later. This plant is useful under trees, either as a ground cover or undergrowth.

● *Aspidistra (Aspidistra elatior)*

The aspidistra is an evergreen perennial with very large leaves, 60 centimeters long by 10 centimeters wide. Although rather tall for an undergrowth plant, it is used to good effect in setting off the low areas of tea gardens and other traditional Japanese gardens. Its flowers, which bloom in spring, are inconspicuous.

○**クサソテツ**

山地の草原や湿地に野生する軟質のシダで，春に出る新葉は巻き込まれ
ていて次第に大きく展開し，薄い羽状に広がる。夏の終りまではその栄
養葉は僅かな風にも揺らぎ，代って冬は茶褐色の堅い胞子葉が立ち，共
に見映えがある。

○**ススキ**

細い葉を四方に開き，高さ１～２ｍに伸びる大きな下草で，秋の七草の
一つとして穂立ちも親しまれている。葉に立縞の入るシマススキ，横斑
が何段も出るタカノハススキ，全体に小柄なイトススキなども用いられ
る。

● **Ostrich fern (*Matteuccia orientalis*)**

This soft fern grows wild on mountain grasslands and in damp
areas. Its new spring fronds are curled at first, eventually
developing into a feather shape. The vegetative leaves sway in
the slightest breeze during the summer. Attractive brown
sporophylls emerge in the winter.

● **Eulalia (*Miscanthus sinensis*)**

The eulalia is one of the traditional "seven autumn flowers." It
is a large undergrowth plant, with spikes and fine leaves growing
1-2 meters in height in all directions. A number of varieties exist,
including those with vertical stripes, horizontal stripes, and
variegations.

ハラン（京都市・実光院）　*Aspidistra elatior*, Jikko-in temple, Kyoto

クサソテツ（神奈川県・大船・乗蓮寺）　Ostrich fern, Joren-ji temple, Ofuna, Kanagawa
prefecture

ススキ（東京都・文京区・小石川後楽園）　Eulalia, Koishikawa Korakuen,
Bunkyo-ku, Tokyo

ススキ（東京都・新宿御苑）　Eulalia, Shinjuku Gyoen National Garden, Tokyo

ヒトツバ（島根県）　*Pyrrosia lingua*, Shimane prefecture

○ヒトツバ

岩上に根茎を長く這わせて厚い卵状披針形の葉を並べて生じる常緑多年草で、葉は切れ込まず1枚ずつが目立ち、この名がある。裏面には胞子が多く付き錆色を呈し、冬には風にそよぎ、緑と茶の彩りを見せる。

○トクサ

水辺の湿地に生じる常緑多年草で、庭では池辺、流れ沿いに用いられ、太さ5mm内外で、50cm以上に緑の円柱状に群生するさまは野趣感が多い。その茎には縦に條が入り、4～5cmおきに黒い節があって、質の硬さを示している。

○ツワブキ

常緑で大きな円形の葉は厚く光沢があり、色も濃くて見映えがして常に庭趣の主役を思わせる。また、花を冬前に黄色く咲かせ、彩るさまも存在力を改めて感じさせてくれる。玄関前など目立つ所に植えて喜ばれる。

● *Pyrrosia lingua*

This evergreen perennial fern grows by creeping along rocks. It has thick, smooth-edged, ovate needlelike leaves arranged in a line. Numerous rust-colored spores grow on the undersurface of the leaves ; when the leaves rustle in the winter wind, the green upper surface and the brownish spores on the underside create an interesting effect.

● **Scouring rush (*Equisetum hyemale*)**

The scouring rush is an evergreen perennial that grows near water ; in gardens it is used along ponds and streams. It grows in clumps, each green, striped stalk measuring about 5 centimeters in thickness and 50 centimeters tall. The stalks are hard, with nodes every 4-5 centimeters. Scouring rushes give a garden a rustic appearance.

● **Japanese silverleaf (*Ligularia tussilaginea*)**

The Japanese silverleaf has large, thick, glossy, orbicular evergreen leaves. Yellow flowers bloom before winter sets in, giving cause for further appreciation of this plant. It is appropriately conspicuous for placement near the entrance to a house.

トクサ（東京都・立川市・国営昭和記念公園）　Scouring rush, Showa Kinen Park, Tachikawa, Tokyo

ツワブキ（仙台市・鶴ケ城）　Japanese silverleaf, Tsuruga-jo castle, Sendai

ギボウシ（埼玉県・川口市立グリーンセンター）　*Hosta undulata Bail* var., Kawaguchi Green Center, Saitama prefecture

○**フキ**

落葉性で，春先には蕗のとうを生じ，葉柄も食すという生活の中で共に暮らすという親愛性のある下草である。葉形はツワブキに似るが，淡緑軟質であり，根茎による発生力もより大きい。

○**シュウカイドウ**

半日陰で湿度のある地に左右非相称の軟かい葉を付ける多年草で，秋には淡紅色４弁の花を開くベゴニアの１種である。そして三つの翼のある実ができ，細かい種子を結び殖えるが，塊状の地下茎や葉腋につく珠芽も繁殖に役立つ。

○**トウギボウシ**

葉長が25〜35cm，幅14〜23cmと大形の葉を開出する多年草で，葉は粉白色のものと緑葉品がある。７月頃，長い花茎を出し，白紫色の花を総状に下から上へと咲かせ続ける。

○**スジギボウシ**

花柄の途中に葉が出るギボウシに近い仲間で，葉は初め何条かの白斑が入り，後には緑化するが，夏には淡紫色の花を開くよく親しまれているギボウシである。斑葉は渋味には欠けるが，庭に賑わしさを与えてくれる。

● **Butterbur (*Petasites japonicus*)**

The leaves of the butterbur resemble those of the Japanese silverleaf, although they are light green and pliable, as well as deciduous. The plant spreads prolifically via rhizomes. After an inconspicuous winter, it sends up its distinctive flower stalks. The leaf stems of the butterbur are used as food.

● **Begonia (*Begonia evansiana*)**

Growing well in moist, partially shaded areas, this variety of begonia is a perennial plant having tender, bilaterally asymmetrical leaves. In the fall it blooms with light crimson four-petaled flowers. Three-winged fruits with fine seeds are produced. The seeds may be planted to grow begonias from scratch, although the bulbils that attached to the plant's axils and large rhizomes may be an easier method of propagation.

● **Plantain lily (var.) (*Hosta*)**

This perennial plant has large leaves, measuring 25-35 centimeters long and 14-23 centimeters wide ; the leaf color may be white or green, depending on the specific variety of plant. Long flower stalks emerge in July, producing light purple flowers in a racemic arrangement, which bloom from down to top. The plant is prominent enough to play a leading role, not a subsidiary one, in the garden.

● **Plantain lily (var.) (*Hosta*)**

This variety of the plantain lily grows leaves along its flower stalks. The leaves start out with white stripes, but eventually turn completely green. Light purple flowers bloom in the summer. The plant adds an element of cheerfulness to the garden.

フキ（京都市・実光院）　Butterbur, Jikko-in temple, Ktoto

シュウカイドウ　*Begonia*

スジギボウシ　Plantain lily

トウギボウシ　Plantain lily

表4．主なる下草類

和 名 ほ か	学　　　名	科　名
カタヒバ	*Selaginella involvens*	イワヒバ
タチクラマゴケ	*S.nipponica*	イワヒバ
クラマゴケ	*S.remotiflora*	イワヒバ
イワヒバ	*S.tamariscina*	イワヒバ
トクサ	*Equisetum hyemale*	トクサ
フユノハナワラビ	*Sceptridium ternatum*	ハナワラビ
ヤシャゼンマイ	*Osmunda lancea*	ゼンマイ
ゼンマイ	*O.japonica*	ゼンマイ
クジャクシダ	*Adiantum pedatum*	イノモトソウ
イワガネゼンマイ	*Coniogramme intermedia*	イノモトソウ
イワガネソウ	*C.japonica*	イノモトソウ
オオバイノモトソウ	*Pteris cretica*	イノモトソウ
タマシダ	*Nephrolepis auriculata*	シノブ
オニヤブソテツ	*Cyrtomium falcatum*	オシダ
ヤブソテツ	*C.fortunei*	オシダ
ベニシダ	*Dryopteris erythrosora*	オシダ
イノデ	*Polystichum polyblepharum*	オシダ
イヌガンソク	*Matteuccia orientalis*	オシダ
クサソテツ	*M.struthiopteris*	オシダ
シシガシラ	*Struthiopteris niponica*	シシガラシ
マメヅタ	*Lemmaphyllum microphyllum*	ウラボシ
ノキシノブ	*Lepisorus thunbergianus*	ウラボシ
ヒトツバ	*Pyrrosia lingua*	ウラボシ
センリョウ	*Chloranthus glaber*	チャラン
フタバアオイ	*Asarum caulescens*	ウマノスズクサ
カンアオイ	*A.nipponicum*	ウマノスズクサ
コバノカンアオイ	*A.variegata*	ウマノスズクサ
ミズヒキ	*Polygonum filiforme*	タデ
フクジュソウ	*Adonis amurensis*	キンポウゲ
ミスミソウ	*Hepatica acuta*	キンポウゲ
バイカイカリソウ	*Epimedium diphyllum*	メギ
イカリソウ	*E.macranthum var.violaceum*	メギ
トキワイカリソウ	*E.sempervirens*	メギ
ハボタン	*Brassica oleracea var.acephala*	アブラナ
オノマンネングサ	*Sedum lineare*	ベンケイソウ
ミセバヤ	*S.sieboldi*	ベンケイソウ
ヤグルマソウ	*Rodgersia podophylla*	ユキノシタ
ユキノシタ	*Saxifraga stolonifera*	ユキノシタ
フッキソウ	*Pachysandra terminalis*	ツゲ
ヒメツゲ	*Buxus microphylla*	ツゲ
ツゲ	*B.m.var.suffruticosa*	ツゲ
イヌツゲ	*Ilex crenata*	モチノキ
ツルマサキ	*Euonymus radicans*	ニシキギ
ハマヒサカキ	*Eurya emarginata*	ツバキ
ヒサカキ	*E.japonica*	ツバキ
チャ	*Thea sinensis*	ツバキ
ゲンジスミレ	*Viola variegata*	スミレ
シュウカイドウ	*Begonia evansiana*	シュウカイドウ
サツキ	*Rhododendron indicum*	ツツジ
アセビ	*Pieris japonica*	ツツジ
マンリョウ	*Ardisis crenata*	ヤブコウジ
カラタチバナ	*A.crispa*	ヤブコウジ
ヤブコウジ	*Ardisia japonica*	ヤブコウジ
シロバナサギゴケ	*Mazus miquelii var.albiferus*	ゴマノハグサ
フイリオオバコ	*Plantago asiatica f.variegata*	オオバコ
ヒトエコクチナシ	*Gardenia jasminoides var.radicans f.simpliciflora*	アカネ
ハクチョウゲ	*Serissa japonica*	アカネ
アサギリソウ	*Artemisia schmidtiana*	キク
ミヤコワスレ	*Aster savatieri*	キク
コギク	*Chrysanthemum morifolium var.sinense f.*	キク
ツワブキ	*Ligularia tussilaginea*	キク
フキ	*Petasites japonicus*	キク
ヤブレガサ	*Syneilesis palmata*	キク
オモダカ	*Sagittaria trifolia*	オモダカ
フウチソウ	*Hakonechloa macra*	イネ
イトススキ	*Miscanthus sinensis var.grancillimus*	イネ
タカノハススキ	*M.s.f.zebrinus*	イネ

ヒメシマダケ	*Pleioblastus chino f.angustifolius*	イネ
オロシマチク	*P.distichus*	イネ
チゴザサ	*P.fortunei*	イネ
カムロザサ	*P.vividi-striatus*	イネ
カサスゲ	*Carex dispalata*	カヤツリグサ
シマカンスゲ	*C.morrowii var.albo-margimata*	カヤツリグサ
ササノハスゲ	*C.pachygyna*	カヤツリグサ
タガネソウ	*C.siderosticta*	カヤツリグサ
セキショウ	*Acorus gramineus*	サトイモ
ウラシマソウ	*Arisaema thunbergii var.urashima*	サトイモ
タチテンモンドウ	*Asparagus pygmaeus*	ユリ
ハラン	*Aspidistra elatior*	ユリ
スズラン	*Convallaria majus var.keiskei*	ユリ
ドイツスズラン	*C.majalis*	ユリ
フイリホウチャクソウ	*Disporum sessile f.*	ユリ
カタクリ	*Erythronium japonicum*	ユリ
オオバギボウシ	*Hosta sieboldiana*	ユリ
ギボウシ	*H.undulata var.erromena*	ユリ
リュウキュウヤブラン	*Liriope gracilis*	ユリ
ヤブラン	*L.graminifolia*	ユリ
ヒメヤブラン	*L.minor*	ユリ
ノシラン	*Ophiopogon jaburan*	ユリ
ジャノヒゲ	*O.japonicus*	ユリ
オオバジャノヒゲ	*O.planiscapus*	ユリ
ヒメイズイ	*Polygonatum humile*	ユリ
アマドコロ	*P.officinale*	ユリ
キチジョウソウ	*Reineckia carnea*	ユリ
オモト	*Rohdea japonica*	ユリ
ツルタイワンホトトギス	*Tricyrtis formosana var.stolonifera*	ユリ
ヒガンバナ	*Lycoris radiata*	ヒガンバナ
スイセン	*Narcissus tazetta var.chinensis*	ヒガンバナ
タマスダレ	*Zephyranthes candida*	ヒガンバナ
ヒメシャガ	*Iris gracilipes*	アヤメ
シャガ	*I.japonica*	アヤメ
イチハツ	*I.tectorum*	アヤメ
エビネ	*Calanthe discolor*	ラン
シュンラン	*Cymbidium virescens*	ラン

索引

●ア行

アオキ	73
アケビ	115
アジュガ	89
アズマネザサ	36,93
アツバキミガヨラン	64
アベリア	35
アラカシ	40
イタビカズラ	113
イヌツゲ	17,28,35,68,69,74
イヌマキ	17,27,38
イノデ	123
ウバメガシ	27
エイザンゴケ	82
オウゴンイトヒバ	61
オウゴンキャラボク	47
オウゴンクジャクヒバ	64
オウゴンコノテガシワ	60
オウゴンタマイブキ	46
オオイタビ	113
オオムラサキツツジ	32
オカメザサ	90
オモト	123
オロシマチク	93

●カ行

カイズカイブキ	24,25,26,55,56,57,65,66,74
カエデ	75
カナメモチ	31
カナリーキヅタ	108
カラタチ	33
カロライナジャスミン	52
カンチク	59
カンツバキ	47,68
キウイ・フルーツ	117
ギボウシ	126
キャラボク	35,42,44,46,68,71
キョウチクトウ	32
キンモクセイ	30
クサソテツ	106,125
クズ	117
クマザサ	91
クロマツ	16
ゲッケイジュ	33
コウライシバ	101
コガネシダ	122
コクマザサ	92,93
コクチナシ	102
コケ	77,83
コシダ	124

コツボゴケ	82
コトネアスター	31,104
コノテガシワ	61
ゴールドクレスト	64

●サ行

サザンカ	78
サツキ	27,40,69,70,74,78
サワラ	25,27
サンゴジュ	19,32
シイ	20
シバ	101
シバザクラ	88
シャガ	103
シュウカイドウ	127
シラカシ	17,18,19,20
シロツメグサ	103
スギゴケ	82,83
スジギボウシ	127
ススキ	125
セイヨウアジサイ	73
セイヨウキヅタ	109
セイヨウツゲ	28,44,45,47,68,70
セイヨウバクチノキ	54
セキショウ	96,99

●タ行

ダイコンドラ→ディコンドラ	
タチカンツバキ	30
タマイブキ	66,67
タマリュウ	96,97,98,99
チゴザサ	92
チャ	39
チョウジカズラ	89,105,114
ツキヌキニンドウ	49
ツゲ	74
ツツジ	47
ツバキ	23,41
ツルニチニチソウ	88
ツルバラ	48
ツワブキ	103,126
テイカカズラ	36,53,114
ディコンドラ	95
トウギボウシ	124
ドウダンツツジ	33,42,46,75
トクサ	119,126
トケイソウ	50

●ナ行

ニオイヒバ	61

ナツヅタ	107,108,109,110,111,113
ナニワイバラ	49
ナリヒラダケ	57,71
ナワシログミ	38
ナンテン	59
ニッコウヒバ	27,43
ノウゼンカズラ	52
ノシバ	100

●ハ行

ハイビャクシン	16,84,85
ハクチョウゲ	44
ハトスヘデラ	116
ハラン	103,124,125
ヒイラギナンテン	63
ヒイラギモクセイ	29,40
ヒサカキ	34,43
ヒトツバ	126
ビナンカズラ	53
ヒマラヤスギ	9,22
ヒマラヤピラカンサ	37
ヒメシマダケ	94
ヒラドツツジ	32,62,63,74
ピラカンサ(トキワサンザシ)	37,75
フイリアメリカツルマサキ	89
フイリチョウジカズラ	114
フイリヤブラン	106,124
フウセンカズラ	52
フウチソウ	123
フキ	127
フクリンツルニチニチソウ	89
フジ	117
フッキソウ	95
ヘデラ	109,110,111,112
ヘデラグレイシャー	112
ヘデラゴールドハート	109
ベニカナメモチ(レッドロビン)	31,47,74
ベニシタン	104
ボケ	34

●マ行

マキ	23,43
マサキ	30
マツバギク	106
マテバシイ	23
マメツゲ	28,45,47,69
ミツバアケビ	115
ミヤギノハギ	58
ミヤマビャクシン	86,87
ムベ	51

メヤブソテツ	122
モチノキ	20,21
モッコウイバラ	49

●ヤ行
ヤブコウジ	102
ヤブツバキ	16
ヤマフジ	116
ヤマモモ	22
ユキノシタ	106
ユキヤナギ	72,73
洋シバ	100
洋種レンギョウ	58

●ラ行
ラカンマキ	26
リュウゼツラン	73
リュウノヒゲ	97,98,99,106

INDEX

A

Abelia(*Abelia grandiflora*) 35
Agave americana Linn. f. 73
Ajuga(*Ajuga*) 89
Akebia trifoliata 115
Algerian ivy(*Hedera canariensis*) 108
Arbortivae(*Thuja occidentalis*) 60
Aspidistra elatior 103, 124, 125
Aucuba(*Aucuba japonica*) 73
Azalea 47

B

Balloon vine 52
Bayberry(*Cedrus deodara*) 22
Begonia(*Begonia evansiana*) 127
Boston ivy(*Parlhenocissus tricuspidata*) 98, 107, 108, 109, 110, 111, 113
Boxwood(*Buxus sempervirens spp.*) 28, 44, 45, 47, 68, 70
Butterbur(*Petasites japonicus*) 127

C

Camellia (Camellia japonica Linne.) 47, 68
Cherokee rose(*Rosa laevigata*) 49
Cherry laurel(*Prunus laurocerasus*) 54
Chinese arborvitae(*Thuja orientalis* Linn.) 61
Chinese black pine(*podcarpus smacrophylla*) 23, 43
Chinese hawthorn(*Photinia glabra*) 31
Chinese juniper shrub(*Juniperus chinensis*) 46, 66, 67
Chinese podocarpus(*Podocarpus chinensis*) 26
Chinese pyramid juniper(*Juniperus chinensis var. kaizuka*) 24, 25, 26, 55, 56, 57, 65, 66, 74
Chinquapin(*Castanopsis Spach.*) 20
Climbing bagbane(*Trachelospermum asiaticum*) 36, 53, 114
Climbing rose(*Rosa spp.*) 48
Coral honeysukle(*Lonicera sempervirens*) 49
Cotoneaster(*Cotoneaster*) 31, 104
Creeping euonymus(*Euonymus fortunei* Hand.) 89
Creeping fig(*Ficus pumila* Linn.) 113
Creeping Japanese juniper(*Juniperus chinensis Linn. var. procumbens*) 61, 84, 85
Creeping saxifrage(*Saxifraga stolonifera*) 106
Cyrtomium fortunei 122

D

Deodar(*Cedrus deodrus*) 9, 22
Dichondra(*Dichondra repens var. carolinensis*) 95
Dicranopteris dichotoma 124
Dwarf cape jasmine(*Gardina jasminoides* Ellis.) 102
Dwarf Japanese snake's beard(*Opiopogon japonicus f. nanus*) 96, 97, 98, 99, 106

E

English ivy 109
Enkianthus perulatus 33, 42, 46, 75
Eulalia(*Miscanthus sinensis*) 125
Euonymus(*Euonymus fortuni "Emerald"*) 89
Eurya japonica 34, 43

F

Ficus foveolata var. nipponica 113
Fringed iris(*Iris japonica*) 103

G

Goldcrest 64
Golden peacock hiba(*Chamaecyparis obtusaendl var.*) 64
Golden biba arborviatae 61
Ground bamboo(*Pleioblastus chino*) 94
Ground bamboo grass(*Pleioblastus chino* Makino) 36, 93

H

Hair moss 82, 83
Hakonechloa macra 123
Hevenly bamboo(*Nandina domestica* Thunb.) 59
Himalayan Pyracantha 37
Hirado azalea(*Rhododendron weyrichii X*) 32, 62, 63, 74
Holm oak(*Cuercus phillyraeoides*) 27
Hosta undulata Bail. var. 126
Hydrangea(*Hydrangea spp.*) 73

I

Ilex(*Ilex integra*) 20, 21
Ivy 116
Ivy(*Hedera rhombea*) 109, 110, 111, 112

J

Japanese black pine(*Pinus thungergii*) 16
Japanese boxtree (*Buxus mycrophlla* Seibe) 74
Japanese camellia(*Camellia japonica* Linn.) 16
Japanese coral tree(*Viburnum awabuki*) 19, 32
Japanese holly(*Ilex crenata*) 17, 28, 35, 68, 69, 74
Japanese littleleaf holly(*Ilex crenata var.*) 28, 45, 47, 69

Japanese lawn grass 101
Japanese mahonia(*Mahonia japonica*) 63
Japanese pachysandra(*Pachysandra terminalis*) 95
Japanese purples(*Lespedega penduliflora*) 58
Japanese quince(*Chaenomeles lagenaria*) 34
Japanese silverleaf(*Ligularia tussilaginea*) 103, 126
Japanese white oak(*Quercus myrsinaefolia*) 17, 18, 19, 20
Japanese wisteria 117
Japanese yew(*Taxus cuspidata var. umbraculifera*) 35, 42, 44, 46, 68, 71

K

Kazura japonica 53
Kiwifruit 117
Kokuma bamboo grass 92, 93
Kuma bamboo grass(*Sasa veitchii* Rehd.) 91
Kuzu vine 117

L

Lampranthus spectabilis 106
Laurel 33
Liriope graminifolia var. 106, 124
Lithocarpus edulis 23

M

Maple tree 75
Marbled bamboo(*Chimonobambusa marmorea*) 59
Mascarenegrass(*Zoysia matrella var. tenuifolia*) 101
Moss 77, 82, 83
Moss pink(*Phlox subulata*) 88

N

Narihira bamboo 57, 71
Nikko sypress(*Chamaecyparis pisifera var. plumosa f.*) 27, 43

O

Okame banboo grass(*Shibataea kumasaca* Makino) 90
Oleander(*Nerium oleander*) 32
Orange fragrant olive(*Osmanthus fragrans*) 30
Osmanthus fortunei 29, 40
Ostrich fern(*Matteuccia orientalis*) 106

P

Passionflower(*Passiflora coerulea*) 50
Periwinkle(*Vinca major var.*) 89
Periwinkle(*Vinca minor*) 88
Plantain lily(var.)(*Hosta undulat Bailey*)

127

Plantain lily(var.)(*Hosta Sieboldiana*) 127
Pleioblastus distichus 93
Pleioblastus fortunei 92
Podocarpus(*Podocarpus macrophylla*) 17,
    27, 38
Polystichum polyblepharcum 123
Pyracantha(*Pyracanthus coccinea*) 37, 75
Pyrrosia lingua 126

R

Red robine(*Photinia glabra f. red robine*)
    31, 47, 74
Rhododedron Omurasaki 32
Ring-cupped oak(*Quercus glauca* Thunb.)
    40
Rock cotoneaster(*Cotoneaster horizontalis*)
    104
Rohdea japonica 123
Rosa banksiae 49

S

Sargent juniper(*Juniperus chinensis* Linn.
    var. sargentii Henry) 86, 87
Sasanqua 78
Satsuki azalea(*Rhododendron indicum*)
    27, 40, 69, 70, 74, 78
Sawara cypress(*Chamaecyparis pisifera*)
    25, 27
Saxifrage stolonifera Meerb 106
Scouring rush(*Equisetum hyemale*) 124
Selaginella remotiflora 82
Serissa japonica 44
Silky wisteria(*Wiateria brachybotrys* seib.)
    116
Spanish dagger(*Yucca gloriosa* Linn.) 64
Spearflower(*Ardisia japonica*) 102
Spindle tree(*Enonymus japonica*) 30
Spirea(*Spiraea thunbergii*) 72, 73
Stauntonia hexophylla 51
Sweet flag(*Acorus gramineus*) 96, 99

T

Tall winter camellia(*Camellia hiemalis*)
    30
Tea(*Thea sinensis*) 39
Thorny elaeagnus(*Elaeagnus Pungens*
    Thunb.) 38
Thuja occidentalis Linn. 61
Trachelospermum saiaticum var. 89, 105,
    114
Trifoliate orange(*Poncirus trifolata*) 33
Trumpet creeper(*Campsis chinensis*) 52

W

Weeping golden bell(*Forsythia suspensa*
    Vahl) 58
White clover(*Trifolium repens*) 103

Winter camellia 47, 68
Woodsia macrochlaena 122

Y

Yellow jessamine(*Gelsemium sempervirens*)
    52

Z

Zoysia(*Zoysia japonica* Steud.) 100
Zoysia(*Zoysia japonica*) 100

あとがき

　生垣とカバープランツを主題とした本書の撮影に際しては，前作『竹垣のデザイン』と同じく情報が少なく，見本となる生垣やグランドカバーの良い例を探すのに苦労しました。樹木の種類や地方の特色がある生垣がもっとたくさんあると思います。いつものことではありますが，もう少し時間があれば，と改めて時間や情報の少なさを嘆くばかりです。しかし，ふだんよく見かける生垣やグランカバーの一般的な植栽例として，なにかの参考にしていただければ本書の目的は達せられるものと，一区切りすることにいたしました。

　出雲の文化財として指定を受けたほどの見事な築地松も，害虫の被害で一本の松さえ残っていないこともありました。あまり身近すぎていつも通っている道の生垣も，花が咲いて初めて気がついたり，いつの間にか生垣が取り払われ，ブロック塀になったりして，寂しさを感じたこともあります。

　ブロックやコンクリート塀を生垣に作り替えることを推奨する自治体が増えてきました。しかし，確実に身のまわりから緑が少なくなっています。改めて生垣の存在，植栽の意義を考えたいと思います。

　近年，樹木の種類が増え，輸入種や交配種が多くなりました。本書に解説をつけてくださった相関芳郎先生にはこの分類でご厄介をお掛けいたしました。深く感謝いたします。また，多数の写真をレイアウト，デザインしてくださいました柳川研一氏，出版に際してご尽力をいただきましたグラフィック社，撮影の際に快く許可をしてくださいました多くの方々に，心からお礼を申し上げます。

鈴木おさむ

相関芳郎（あいぜき　よしろう）
1920年，東京浅草生まれ。
東京都の公園・庭園・霊園などの植栽と管理に従事。
神代植物公園所長などを歴任して退職。
著書に『雑木と下草』（主婦と生活社・共著）などが
ある。

鈴木おさむ（すずき　おさむ）
1943年，中国瀋陽生まれ。
福岡大学法学部卒業後，千代田写真専門学校に学ぶ。
アパレル・メーカー宣伝部を経て現在はフリーラン
スの写真家として活動。
著書に『竹垣のデザイン』（グラフィック社・共著）
などがある。

生垣とカバープランツ

1997年 7月25日　初版第1刷発行

写　真	鈴木おさむ	発行所　グラフィック社
文	相関芳郎	〒102 東京都千代田区九段北1-9-12
発行者	久世利郎	電話 03-3263-4318
写　植	三和写真工芸株式会社	Fax 03-3263-5297
印刷所	恒美印務有限公司	振替・00130-6-114345
製本所	恒美印務有限公司	

ISBN4-7661-0973-2 C3071